MINORITIES AS
COMPETITIVE OVERLORDS

MINORITIES AS COMPETITIVE OVERLORDS

Jimanze EgoAlowes

Safari Books Ltd
Ibadan

Published by

Safari Books Ltd
Ile Ori Detu
1, Shell Close
Onireke
Ibadan.
Email: info@safaribooks.com.ng
Website: http://safaribooks.com.ng

In Association with

The Stone Press Limited
P.O. Box 5681, Festac Town, Lagos
Email: *thestonebooks@yahoo.com*

First Published 2017

ISBN: 978-978-54785-1-8

DEDICATION

For Chief F.O. Offia, LLB (Hons), BL
A great lover of Truth and the Arts.

TABLE OF CONTENTS

PART ONE

Part Two

Part Three

Postscript

PREFACE

This work by Jimanze Ego-Alowes makes a fascinating and compelling read. The author shares an uncommon and thought-provoking perspective on the subject matter which is at once refreshing, enthralling and fundamental. He argues strongly that this is the best time to be a minority in a competitive dog-eat-dog environment and that the minorities, because of the peculiarities of their existence, are generally talented and have a natural competitive advantage, which, when understood, appreciated and effectively deployed, represents a strong, strategic characteristic business asset.

He illustrates and adumbrates his thesis with the examples of the minority's almost wholesale dominance of the media and banking businesses in Nigeria. He argues rather convincingly that it is the dynamics of the sociology and changing pattern of that sociology that confers this existential prowess on the minorities. He goes further to posit that the minorities have inherent dividends and other compensating assets attached to their number deficit which the author defines as the 'the brace factor advantage'; that in the particular Nigerian situation, while the big tribes of Igbo, Hausa/Fulani and Yoruba constitute the three legs of the Nigerian tripod, the South-South represents the ring that connects or braces them together. He argues further that since these majority players all want to be really regional, while pretending to be national for political correctness, that the nearest people to a national and nationalistic group are the South-Southerners.

He illustrates further this thesis of the sociology of business and the advantages it automatically confers with much conviction by focusing on such varied areas of business endeavors such as the mass movement of people by buses, the humour business and events management. In the humour business, he pointedly reaches the conclusion, which could be controversial, that the most creative people are the minorities. And that to create and to be most creative in the humour business it is generally recognized that one needs to be a minority as great humour is the inheritance of the doomed and sorrowful and that history confirms this assertion.

This work contains some rather theoretical postulations which could engage another author who might want to challenge and interrogate them in some other contexts or milieu. Some of the assertions had the effect on me as that of coming into a sudden awareness and realization of some facts regarding the existential realities of Nigeria. This opus comes well recommended to all those who are in search of knowledge and fundamental truths underpinning the realities of life in Nigeria which could be deployed to gain competitive advantage. But it is only fair to warn that the style of presentation, the language and the inherent logic are far from pedestrian.

-Dr. Boniface Chizea (Lagos, 2013)

-Jimanze EgoAlowes
Queen Mother A'Endu Fortress, Oru Nkwerre. July 2014.

Introductory Remarks And Definitions

The general trust of the essays is to establish a thesis that there is what we call Sociology of Business Turf Advantage. Its specific thesis is to document an economic position that minorities are not in competitive environments as under-privileged as they may readily appear. In fact, the essay canvasses that if the minorities or so-called marginal parties court knowledge they did turn up competitive overlords. Perhaps this is the best time to be a minority in a competitive world.

The assumption, however, is that it is a multi-party competitive environment and that the parties are of variant sizes, which is a typical environment. That is to say, there are majority and minority parties so defined. The definition of majority and minority parties could be on the basis of population which is only one measurement. Other endowments could also make one a majority or minority or so-called marginal party. But in these studies we are concerned with population asset definitions.

By 'sociology of business' is meant the dynamic that generates economies of achievement or business success, not because of the innate abilities of a given group or individuals within that group. Sociology of business is in the configuration(s) inherent in the competitive parties' displacements in space, time and assets. And we recognise that these configurations are not fixed. They move and change, even if not as frequently as to be an ogbanje or abiku. So in the moments or years they last, the understanding of their nature is in itself an unbeatable competitive asset.

So in a Nigerian case study, the minorities are not assumed to be more or less talented. The thesis is that they will have natural comparative advantage issuing, as it were, from the disadvantage or weakness in numbers. The important thing is to understand this and deploy the understanding as a strategic asset and comparative tool. There are niche businesses and competitive areas they would be quick to trounce all non-minority, all majority competitors, despite what appears on the face of it as disadvantages.

PART ONE:

1

Why and how Nigerian media moguls... are all from the South-South minority

The day is coming when a single carrot, freshly observed, will set off a revolution.... **(Paul Cezanne)**

Were it not for the Nigerian-Biafran Civil War, it is almost certain that neither Raymond Dokpesi of Ray Power/ AIT, John Momoh of Channels TV, Ben Murray Bruce of Rhythm Radio/Silverbird TV, on one hand, nor Sam Amuka of Vanguard, Alex Ibru of The Guardian, Nduka Obiagbena of ThisDay, Frank Aigbogun of BusinessDay, on the other, would have been the successful media moguls that they are in the print or electronic formats today! Or, if they had insisted on being media men, they would not have in any way achieved the dominant positions they command today.

Their dominant ownership, control and reach of the Nigerian media are not an accident of geography or a conspiracy of South-South irredentists, as has sometimes been foolishly and ignorantly canvassed. It is, simply put, a dynamic of the sociology and changing patterns of that sociology. It is that sociology, as it is presently constituted or stabilised, that has made these great South-Southerners media top-dogs, in spite of, rather than because of themselves or their gifts.

The incontestable supposition is that they are great men in their own weights as is shown by the big ticket achievement of the businesses they run, which only happen to be about

1

media assets today. But if the sociology of business had not warranted it they would have found some other home-advantage terrains and market niches for themselves. Man, as an evolutionary animal, is in search of his best evolutionary habitats, whether it is in business, marriage and political alliances. That he is not consciously aware of this does not deprecate the fact.

Perhaps, these media men would have incarnated as philosophers, mathematicians, ship merchants, etc. Just like Zie Alowesteins, a local wag, once conjectured, if Einstein was born in the Jerusalem of Christ, he could have turned up a prophet, and not mathematical-physicist. We are all children of our fathers, as we are of our times.

It is true that one can always outgrow his past or background. However, a complementary truth is that his background is the only position from which he may take off. A runner, say a Usain Bolt, who bests the world's records, has to start from the blocks. He can't start from the finishing line. That is the very logic of being. The past is a garrison from which one may escape into future frontiers. But he begins from that past or the blocks which incidentally shapes his trajectory and all too probably the distance he may go.

Sociology Is Not Ethnic

Before we go a line further, let us state unequivocally that sociology is a wholly human creation and not an inheritable gene. Sociology is not a tribe and is not ethnic, although ethnics have their sociology which is just about the same as having their own geography. Yes, they do, but people migrate and lose their old geography or sociology and acquire new ones. The Americans, who all came from Europe and other continents and the Jews, are ready examples.

The fact that sociology is wholly human means it is a changeling and can be acquired, perhaps over time. And events, especially acts of God, can so radically and on short notice alter the configuration of a people. One of such events is the Nigerian-Biafran Civil War, which came with a sociological importation we as Nigerians have refused to study or address.

It is not entirely an African thing. The World War II, made Germans, an eternally warlike tribe, from the Swabian Dynasty emperors to Hitler, now one of Europe's greatest peace-mongering nations. It is the American Civil War, more than anything else, that made the Americans who they that are; it gave them a new and, if one liked, a self-elect sociology. Before then America was just another Canada or New Zealand, and would have so remained, one can conjecture. The war altered the sociology of the Americans and they came to their own for the first time and matured in that light. The Jews again are a people whose shifting sociological fortunes have altered them into the world's premier reservoir of human genius. These, of course, have sociology of business and even other implications which is, perhaps, not within the remit of this essay.

The contention of this essay is that the "sociology of business advantage" is a necessary though not a sufficient condition for profit and loss or entrepreneurial success. Without it no great enterprises can be built and sustained in business, sciences and sports. And it explains the cluster of successes that one finds in Silicon Valley, Onitsha, etc. It is not mysterious and can, with painstaking attention, be reversed, engineered and understood.

The truth and fact, as they stand today, are that the sociology of business advantage of the media is on the credit of and leans towards the side of the South-South, a minority zone of the Nigerian nation. It will thus serve our greatest purpose if we understood this formally, rather than anecdotally or even refuse to understand and take it as a given as a falling apple, before Isaac Newton visited. A formal appreciation will suggest to stakeholders and competitors what next will be the best step and how.

THE MATTHEW EFFECT

Before we go to the details, it may be proper to remark that the 'Mathew Effect' also plays to the favour of the sociology of business advantage. To whom much is given much is expected. Big and enduring business and life successes are often built on just one advantage identified and exploited. With that one advantage, one reaches a critical mass and by his success, invites others who can bring in other assets and advantages and add to the original or originating one. That is, one success invites newer successes. Ikea furniture, great innovation, was in flat parking of furniture and Wal-Mart chose to contend with more established competition, and beat them, like Mao once did, from the non-metropolitan areas. Peace Mass Transit, Nigeria, started to cover poor commuters, with affordable fares on cheap and ready Chinese bus brands. And by the time the firm's competitors knew, the start-up was as big as they are. Of course, the firm is now diversified into several other businesses manned by hired competent hands. Today, Peace Mass Transit is a brand name that commuters and the larger community bank on.

This little start up advantage, which could be or have been, sociology of business, cash, location, etc, advantage, generates a certain logic or momentum, that includes the capacity to hire the best hands and a supportive growth of federating sub-contractor industries that will help sharpen the saw and beat off prospective competitors. Sub-contractors are a source of product innovation that the Japanese experience has proved in bold relief, over and over in their business.

Immediately this threshold of Mathew Effect is achieved the industry takes a life as a cluster or network of spaces; Silicon Valley, Onitsha, Diaspora Jews, ethnic Chinese Diaspora, or the South-Southerners. At this point, the cluster or network of space or dispersed entrepreneurs will have acquired a life of its own and is unbeatable. That is, the industry and the geography, the dance and the dancer, become one and are unbeatable, except at high levels of precision or competitive counter-attack. And this comes in the form of changing the ground rules, by exclusively patented technology say, which is a black swan event. Silicon Valley presently is an unbeaten and unbeatable innovation garden. Onitsha was before coordinated and still largely running anti-South-East/Igbo policies hit her. Perhaps, in some diminished form Onitsha still is.

Today, one can say that the South-South media moguls and the Nigerian media are about achieving this threshold; that is, they are becoming unbeatable and this is likely to remain so for a long time. This is what accounts for their dominance and not any media conspiracy. It is a scientific thing. Just a little inquiry and we would come to understand it.

How the South-South Acquired the Sociology of Business Advantage

The media are a curious asset. They are in a very unique position almost like no other. Nothing we can conjecture quite compares to the media. They require the especially talented to produce their content. That is, the media are forms of art. Perhaps, this is universally acknowledged and needs no illustrations. But we will give one anyway. Commonly in Nigeria today, a journalist like Dele Giwa could be a household name as a star even while he was a paid staff of Daily Times and had little else to his fame. In fact, he was so independently famous that a co-employee journalist, Mee Ezekiel, rated him a better dressed celebrity than MKO Abiola, their employer at the Concord newspapers.

The media are also power-measuring meters. They are projectiles of power and a state's defence and repair mechanism. This is obvious both in free and open societies as it is in closed and communist dictatorships. While in open societies it is not very apparent, it is in communist societies. Usually, the ownership and control of the media in all dictatorships are wholly in the hands of the government in power. That the state or the dictatorship wholly owns and runs the media is a commentary on the absence of the plurality of powers, opinions or influences.

Let us use a contemporary example. On June 30, 2012, the Economist of London reported as follows: "So one can only imagine the consternation caused by yesterday's sensational expose by Bloomberg, which details the financial assets belonging to the family of China's president-in-waiting, Xi Jinping. Bloomberg was careful to note that no part of their investigation directly implicated Mr Xi, his wife, herself a famous PLA officer-cum-singer, Peng Liyuan, or their daughter, who is reportedly studying at Harvard University under an assumed name. The Bloomberg report suggests that other close relatives of Mr Xi have been blessed with abundant good fortune, to put it mildly. The article ties Mr Xi's sister, Qi Qiaoqiao, her husband Deng Jigui, and another brother-in-law, Wu Long, to assets worth hundreds of millions of dollars, or even billions. Their holdings are reported to include stakes in real estate and telecommunications, as well as the sensitive business of producing rare-earth minerals."

It is often speculated that families of officials at all levels of Chinese government are benefiting financially from their access to power. In a country where even a state newspaper "argues in favour of allowing a moderate amount of corruption", should it come as a shock if some of the people in power seek to monetise their positions through favours and largesse?"

To understand the power game in the report, one needs to take cognisance of the fact that Bloomberg is an American media brand and is free about China as it can be. Meanwhile, by the exclusive control of the Chinese traditional media and censorship of the new media, the party operatives are reported in their media as self-sacrificial comrades who are leading China to her status as a world power. The very control of all that the people know is important to the Chinese and all leadership, and that is one way of keeping the citizenry in a state of knowledge that will grant the leadership the most power and the people the least awareness. The critical point is that the media are deployed by Chinese and other governments to prompt citizens to be loyal and law abiding rather than being protesters at the barricades. All governments prefer to see their citizens at the beaches, factories, etc, and not at the picketing lines.

We may all remark quite correctly that without the internet, the Arab Spring, so-called, would not have been possible. The internet opened the vistas and thus the people's eyes to the state of their own very existence, something that was hitherto denied them by the control of the media by interested parties sympathetic to sitting tyrannies. Immediately control slipped beyond the hands of their dictators and tyrants a new order was demanded or put in place.

Indeed, it is not a wholly communist and or dictatorship grip. All powers are quite sensitive to the media. And one illustration suggests the insistence and hypocrisy of open societies. The West, led by America, has been accusing the former Soviet Union of jamming their radio signals to the Soviet people. And it so happened that during the reign of Mikhail Gorbachev, he called for openness, and agreed to look into the issue with Ronald Reagan. During the negotiations he agreed to the history of jamming Western short wave radio signals, which was then popular with the Soviets; then the Russians did not have FM stations. However, he argued quite constructively that Americans, unlike Russians, are tuned to their FM stations just as the Russians to the short waves. It therefore made sense, he proposed, to grant Russians local licence to broadcast FM signals in America, while the Americans will now be allowed to broadcast, un-jammed, into Russia. Reagan, an apostle of open society, abandoned further talks on the cross-matched option. (See Mutual Radio Talks, by Gwynne Dyer, syndicated by New Nigerian – January 9, 1987).

Why? The very presence of Soviet media will constitute, not just an information asymmetry, but a sharing of information space and therefore power. And that could lead to an unsavoury or further loss of power. One loss of power prompts another.

But it is the Iraqi war that provided the most dramatic moment on the loss of media as a power game. The most memorable magic moment of the triumph of Bush against Sadaam Hussein was when the towering image of Sadaam was pulled down. All Western media showed and showed it to no end.

Now, it is not that the showing was not gratuitous; in fact, it was the most visible sign of the power play. But to understand it well we may need to go back to history. Before the invention of the modern media, despots, emperors and potentates also exhibited and communicated their powers in the best way they could. One of it was through currency coinages. And the trickster question against Christ in the Bible is cognate illustration. What face do you have on the coin? (See Mark 1213-17).

What Caesar is saying by the minting of the transactional medium, the currency, available to Christ and others, is that, 'I am the potentate here and you trade and be only by my leave. It is I who grant you the power to be, to trade and to prosper'. And Christ understood it. If he had not acknowledged Caesar upon whose name all Roman citizens may be and prosper, he would indeed be made a prisoner.

So, at any one time, there is a race; an arms race for power. It therefore follows that there is also a race for the instruments of protecting, preserving and perpetuating that power. And one of the most serviceable and proficient instruments outside the business of actually shedding blood is the media. The media are the Abram's tank of democratic warfare, a part of what is today called soft power and also a key arm of their delivery systems. In open societies, in peace and democracy, the media are a theatre of war to contending powers.

The media is the boots on the grounds; the frontier soldiers. While the majority-persons' media are in pitched and fixed positions, the minority-persons' position is to bring antagonists to the round table, which is not a self-sacrificial adventure of the minority media, but in their very best interest, to get the talking go on. The minority acquires its greatest power by mediating two or more superpowers.

LESSONS FROM THE WEST

In Wes0tern societies, including America, the media are especially the business of private business persons or independent publicly funded corporations, like the BBC. It has to be understood that this is an attempt to make the government not constitute an overbearing or dominant or majority-persons' power centre beyond what the victory at the polls permits. The elected governments must, as contenders of power and influence, be prevented from accumulating further power or influence, of playing Caesar. They must be stopped from acquiring the boots to cross the Rubicon, and march against common citizens or other contenders of power and influence. The willed dismissal of governments in Western societies from owning any media platforms is the political/media/structural equivalent of a constitutional monarchy. An elected president with a powerful or dominant media is a monarch. Governments should be dismissed from owning or controlling any media assets at all since they could turn any media asset into a dominant voice in no time with their power and wealth. That a Western government is not allowed to own media is not a matter of morality but that of power play.

On this ground, elected or sitting government will not confuse or conflict the needs of those who are presently in power with the needs of the motherboard, the citizenry or other power contending society-blocs, as the China and other dictatorships exemplify. We must emphasise that the American attempt or media configuration is not just a moral or decency compact but a power game. It is a constitutional compact and structural construction. Its great aim is to so disperse power in such a way that no one bloc, however temporarily triumphant, becomes a domineering or dominant power. Consequently, instead of having an elected American president turn up a Caesar by marching against the Americans, he is denied the media, a source of projecting that power or acquiring the boots to cross the Rubicon.

The logic is that the press and her holders in a free society should be an independent power while the elected also should constitute an independent power source. The two should not be allowed to achieve a combination and formation like the German military did with their infantry, armoured and air corps to enact a blitzkrieg against and overrun the citizenry or state itself.

NIGERIAN SOCIOLOGY OF MEDIA HISTORY

To fully understand the history and geographical dispersal of Nigerian media houses, the following have to be taken into account. Nigeria was a colonial establishment. Before the British came, Nigeria was a land area of different peoples and kingdoms, with little or no administrative or political contact with one another. Despite the assumptions of present day misguided or ignorant patriots, the evidence shows that we had little meaningful contact with one another before the British came. One of the reasons is not that we are xenophobic or culturally asymmetrical, but that we were technically and technologically ill-equipped to meet one another, to cross the Niger, the oceans, and share embraces, as it were. The inability to construct highways, thoroughfares and navigable sea lanes, etc, to connect one another is the single major reason. Even Uthman Dan Fodio's mutinous overthrow of host Hausa kingdoms was stopped on its tracks by his technical inability to construct roads. Unlike the Romans, Dan Fodio and lieutenants simply lacked the ability to build roads or even cross the seas. Perhaps, the River Niger would have drowned them. They could only gallop on their horses on grass and desert lands. That alone precludes the logic of interaction of people. Simply put, the distance and confluence of interaction then was direly limited.

However, the British brought us together by the logic of common colonisation, but more importantly, the construction of motor ways and railways did the magic. Consequently, we came as strangers to live together with one another. The great examples of the Nnamdi Azikiwe and Odumegwu Ojukwu and their Zungeru and Gold Coast, present-day Ghana connections are sufficient testimonies. The two great men were born or grew up in the same Zungeru town and Azikiwe had entrepreneurial seasons in the Gold Coast. It was simply a technical impossibility for Azikiwe/Ojukwu's ancestors to sojourn to Zungeru before the white man's arrival.

But a wind of change was blowing through and it was the wind of change of decolonisation. And we were generally agreed we all needed to be free of our British masters. So the goodwill was initially there on the side of all participating nationalities, who found in the British a common enemy or oppressor. And we were one because we had a common enemy.

This goodwill resulted in the common stand of the elites of the day and their media. But as the details of getting power came, the crack became obvious - that we were never one organic people and that it is the British that brought us together for their imperial purpose.

Part of it may be that the British, who did not want to give away the colony, might have also stoked the differences amongst our hitherto contacts-free peoples to lengthen their over-lordship. The British particularly informed the Northerners that they would be swamped in a new federation in which the Southerners had all the aces as to the emergent federal manpower and employment configurations. Of course, this, in practical terms, might have meant the administrative and consequential domination of the North by the more educated and more Westernised Southerners. It was, of course, true that the North was affected by manpower deficits and needed assurances. This led to the foundation for mutual suspicion. Are we one composite or one unitary Nigeria? This is a question that still haunts us in various guises.

The pre-independence media, of course, were weighted by this sociology of business threats and opportunities. Perhaps, it is understandable that Nigerians then, under the illusion or dominant view of being one people or fighting to sack one common enemy, put on their best nationalistic behaviours. Consequently, the projection of power by the media was by all intents and purposes national and, where it falls short on this, it was more a failure of the heart than the mind. The story of Azikiwe is perhaps illustrative of this.

Those were their greatest days of being nationalists. But the devil is always in the details. And this devil appeared in the rites and rituals of translating the philosophy of being one people into actionable programmes of sharing political or elective offices and posts.

Though the early signs were there but the going of the colonialists showed the cracks or lines of cleavage in bolder relief. It happened, for instance, that Azikiwe and Obafemi Awolowo were contesting in the Western Region and against expected results Awolowo won on the House, as members crossed carpet, abandoning Azikiwe and defecting to support and align with Awolowo.

Azikiwe, in an ill-considered move, committed what most count as one of his greatest political blunders. It was in itself a grave blunder. However, it perhaps would have been more forgivable, if truly as we did believe, we were all one. To make it to the House, Azikiwe raced back to the East, his ancestral home and pushed Eyo Ita from his seat. He thus became less a father of all and was in it for the feathering of his own electoral and power nest. The matter was even made worse by the fact that Eyo Ita was not Igbo, Azikiwe's tribe, but of the Efik nationality. The affront by Azikiwe would have been most pardonable if Eyo Ita was not just an Easterner, a mere geographical classification, but also an Igbo, the ethnic nationality of Azikiwe. But he was not and he rightly thought it was his tribe, he being an Eastern minority tribe, which did him in.

That Azikiwe would have sacked him all the same, if he were Igbo, does not really matter. The fact is that he was not Igbo and Azikiwe's action emphasised that. These easily showed the crack, and that the men as mere mortals were in it for themselves, and possibly, too, for their tribes.

Perhaps, it is the cross-carpeting that hinted at the tribal consciousness and conspiracy. Sometimes Awolowo has been wrongly accused, I suppose, of introducing tribalism into Nigerian politics on account of this. This was the watershed, or the Rubicon that the Nigerian media had to cross to have their empire and territories formally altered and fixed. That is, as the colonialists left and the natives had to take up the reins of power, the nation necessarily degenerated into a cluster of tribes or ethnic nationalities jostling for the power game. Nigeria's political parties became the tribes or a coalition of tribes in effect, even as they bore, nominally, other names like Action Group, NCNC, NPC.

To quote Dayo Duyile in his Makers of Nigerian Press; 'this period saw the birth of the Nigerian Tribune, 1949. This was Chief Obafemi Awolowo's greatest contribution to development of journalism in Nigeria. With his political party's chain of provincial dailies, he competed with Zik's (Azikiwe's) group. One can say, hypothetically, that it was the formation of this chain of newspapers that sustained Dr. Azikiwe and Awolowo for a long time in their national political adventures, political campaigns and which promoted their political beliefs and political plans for Nigeria which emerged in the sixties'.

In the 1960s, the dominant media owners and media were the several governments and the big politicians/businessmen behind them. They were all preaching to the converted. The North with New Nigerian came at about 1966 to join as one and preach its own gospel. Its purpose, like other contender-political blocs, was to secure and possibly project their viewpoints and territory against long range or internal marauders.

So, if the war and coup had not come, the newspapers would still be regional just like you have it in America. And more importantly, no majority ethnic and power group and bidders will leave the education and enlightenment of its voters, captive voters, for whatever reasons, in the hands of a minority people, whose intentions and designs, as with all, are not only undecipherable but never to be trusted. Political exigency would, if necessary, have trumped the market. A market is not, and does not own a polity or country, but a polity has and owns markets.

In the USA, there truly are no national political newspapers. The newspapers are regional and cater to the politics of the localities. The only exception is the Wall Street Journal which is strictly a business daily, and money has no geography or ethnicity. And it is, of course, a notorious fact that business men are pledged to no known nationality. Even Mitt Romney has a great deal of his wealth parked in offshore cash havens, even as he pretends to be a super American patriot. By being rich, you seem to have achieved, if not being a citizen of the world, at least a citizen of your world. A businessman's allegiances are to his balance sheet and not the national pledge. If it is more profitable, I can assure, a Dangote, or an Anyaehie will quit Nigeria to live in just any other haven, even if it be hell.

The reasons America has no national newspapers are at bottom the reasons we once did. It is just that the currencies of expression vary no less than the dollar and naira. But all are moneys, means of exchange, of intra-border and inter-person interaction. America, we can quickly remind ourselves, is built as the pyramid, from ground up. Regional and state and even individual powers are so structured; it is the closest you can come to confederation. So the states are not dependent on Washington, our own Abuja, and do not want to be. And there is no too big a deal in being of Washington, unlike of being Abuja. In fact, American presidents are more powerful abroad than at home and this is by its studied political architecture or design.

But the coup changed the sociology of Nigerian newspapering and much else in Nigeria. Expectedly, in the heady days of the coup the newspapers prevaricated. But immediately the war started Daily Times and New Nigerian were as gung ho against the Igbo/East as the soldiers. A Daily Trust writer, Mahmud Jega, on November 28, 2011, recalls it all, even as he restricts reminisces to the radio. The point is that the Federal media was deployed in a campaign of demonization of the other, who is hell. We quote, "Ojukwu was by then the number one hate figure in Nigeria, the loyalist part of it. Ojukwu bashing dominated the early years of our lives in the late 1960s. The Nigerian Army composed many songs against Ojukwu and Biafra, which were played on the radio every day."

While the soldiers carried the guns, Daily Times/New Nigeria carried the pen and they all acted as one in the murder and justification of murder. Of New Nigerian, no one expected anything less. But the least showing of independence by Daily Times and further northern irredentism by New Nigeria, which apparently did not know the war had ended, incurred their nationalisation by the Murtala/Obasanjo military junta. It also has to be understood that being unelected and in some sense unelectable dictators, these men of guns, mayhem and violence needed to seize the press to protect, preserve and project the power they stole through coup.

It is instructive perhaps that these newspapers represented the wining power bloc configuration of the North and the West, which for the coup makers, was all the country amounted to. For them, the East was a defeated people and the minorities were of no real consequence. And already in the guise of nationalism, which really meant exclusively consolidated Northern and Western interests, the oil wells in the South-South and the East were seized. And they were later used to build up Lagos and Abuja, even as the East/Igbo and the oil rich minority South-South were abandoned as economic wastelands.

And like a British seasoned editor said of all power newspapers, these papers, that is New Nigerian and Daily Times, were strictly not readable. They all broadly were in league with the dictatorship of the day, which served their purpose and those of the Nigerian-style two Security Council regions of the North and the West, and strafed the rest of the nation. All they did was to once in a while pick a friendly quarrel with the government. Daily Times and New Nigeria were like rocket drones in the hand of the military to frighten and condition the populace with lies, fraud and propaganda and project the power of the evil dictators. The dilapidating public ineptitude in Nigeria today is in a great measure the work of Daily Times and New Nigerian. They are all gone or nearly so, but the evil they did lives after them.

Let us quote Sir Peregrine Worsthorne, editor of London Sunday Telegraph (1986-1989). In his essay 'Dumbing Up' in The Penguin Book of Journalism, edited by Stephen Glover (Penguin 1999), he writes: "As for leading articles, these too were intended to help rather than hinder. The king's government had to be carried on, and although this did not preclude constructive criticism, or even partisan criticism, it precluded criticism which might endanger the national interest. Hence the conspiracy agreed upon by all the British newspapers of the time, left-wing as well as right-wing, to conceal from the public, until the very last moment, Edward VIII's scandalous liaison with Wallis Simpson.

In those days, it has to be remembered, Britain was still a great power, with a great empire, the hub of the universe, with the kind of quality newspapers that such all-important role required. If you want to know what they read like, start taking the New York Times, which is the nearest equivalent today. Nobody would read it for pleasure. It is painfully dull, badly written, prolix and boring, full of details, domestic and foreign-unabridged G-7 communiqués for example- which no contemporary British newspapers would any longer dream of printing, for fear of boring readers into cancelling their subscriptions.... New York Times readers, like London Times readers in the old days, do not feel they are getting their money's worth unless they are bored, rather as patients do not feel medicine is doing them any good unless it tastes nasty.

Thank heavens that it has no longer been the case here in Britain for many years. For with the end of Britain's Great Power responsibilities, even the most educated newspaper readers began to look for gossip rather than for news, for pleasure rather than for business, for speculation rather than for facts-and above all for human interest stories rather than for public interest stories".

In those days, whether or not it was known to the duo of the North and the West, the twin or joint winners of the Civil War, their interests were in building a great empire, with them as the British of Nigeria. They ran Nigeria like an empire and thus originating all or nearly all our post-Civil War problems. From Gowon to Murtala, no New Nigerian or Daily Times editorial and reporter ever wrote a line on oil spillage. Yet they all gathered over the open graves and despoliation of the oil-bearing regions to build Lagos and Abuja into mega cities. As at today, individuals from these two ethnic groups own more oil per capita and in unattached numbers than all the South-South peoples. Can one really imagine the South-South indigenes owning the majority of groundnut pyramids or cocoa lots in Kano or Oyo before the war, or even now if the business were to be resuscitated? Yet this is the reverse logic of what happens over oil and Daily Times and New Nigerian kept their dubious peace and criminal silence.

With the empire building newspapers of Daily Times and New Nigerian unable to build any real empire in collusion with the military, the cracks became visible despite the dust raised by the guns and drumbeats of the newspapers, editors, reporters, etc, on hire. The military, despite their claims of nationalistic credentials, were as tribal, as sectional and partisan as the devil and not even their rented or owned media could tell any believable lies again. Their partisan actions were deafeningly loud and could not be contradicted by verbal logic.

THE LOCAL POST-WAR INDEPENDENT PRESS

The first real newspaper The Punch that made the rounds was founded by Sam Amuka, a South-South minority man and editor. The Punch was financed by Olu Aboderin, a business man and Westerner. They later had issues and Amuka pulled out and founded Vanguard which was also a hit. Then came The Guardian which was founded by Stanley Macebuh/Dele Smart Cole, South-Southerners and financed by Ibru, another South-Southerner. Macebuh, though nominally Igbo, must be understood as an expatriate Easterner/Igbo. He had the best of America in him; that is, he assigned no weight as to provenance, where you are or born into. Apparently, what mattered to him was where you were going. And this being Nigeria and not America, we all saw how far he really went.

Now, outside Daily Sun, the dominant newspapers with national coverage and followership are The Guardian, Vanguard, ThisDay and The Punch almost in that order. The papers themselves refuse to acknowledge any circulation transparencies or figures. The Punch may, even if we believe her propaganda, outsell them each, but its readership is concentrated in Lagos/Southwest area and puts a question mark on its pan-national circulation and other credentials. Of course, the rest, owned and controlled by the South-Southerners, dwarf The Punch which is the Southwest's (owned) most successful media asset, or The Daily Trust and Leadership, both the North's leading media assets. The failure of New Nigerian and The Punch's success can also be later explained by the sociology of business in another paper. (I write a column at The Sun and have to exclude it as much as I can from this paper and analysis, for reasons of fairness and balance. However it is germane to remark that The Sun fits perfectly, and is explainable within the sociology of business models).

NOW WHAT MAKES MEDIA SUCCESSFUL?

I think the greatest response was given by Diana Vreeland, the imperial lady who ruled and reigned as editor-in-chief of Vogue and we quote from her memoirs DV: "I think part of my success as an editor came from never worrying about (1) a fact, a cause, and an atmosphere. It was me projecting to the public. That was my job. (2) I think I always had a perfectly clear view of what was possible for the public. (3) Give 'em what they never knew they wanted.

(And we comment; this is what makes for the media an art work almost unique to the editor or publisher. That is, to decipher what the boys are so hungry for, even as they are gorging themselves on the wrong meals and give them the greatest literary feast of their lives. And they will have a fresh lease, perhaps release of life as they never knew they can have).

(1) And you must not be projecting me, or as relevant in Nigeria, a particular or particularistic or hidden agenda. Or if you are, you better not be caught or even be suspected.

(2) The ability or position to seem and or be a third and independent party; that is, the media for exchange of ideas and contest among contending blocs. A fair playing ground, which is what a given model media should be for antagonists.

(3) The media must achieve the ability to be, if not supportive of the ruling classes, then at least no visible enemy, of theirs. As Karl Marx puts it, the ideas of the ruling class are in every epoch the ruling ideas. That is, it must be understood that the ruling class would not wish another warfront to be opened in the media and against it, if it can afford it. This explains why Alex Ibru was appointed Minister of Internal Affairs in the first place. It was to co-opt The Guardian, a fairly powerful medium, on the side of the dictator, General Sani Abacha. Ibru was naïve and thought he was something of a geek. The Abacha people did not need his genius, if he had any; they needed his co-conspiracy. They wanted him as partner in the crime of politically looting a nation, not because he is the best brain in town, but because it will be one enemy front eliminated. Or perhaps, a potential foe or power-competitor turned an ally.

And when then President Olusegun Obasanjo got too hot and uncomfortable with Orji Kalu, he sent in a special media audit squad to comb The Sun and possibly close it. Kalu, allegedly, is the promoter of The Sun. And luckily they did not find any smoking gun, and the rest is history. It is not that Obasanjo hates Kalu, though that is not outside all Obasanjo can do. No, it is rather that Obasanjo would not want a powerful tool aimed at, or which at any time might be aimed or co-opted to be aimed at him, to prosper.

(4) There is also need for a captive market. In the U.K., the U.S. and the West generally, it is defined by literacy and

target audience and socio-economic bulge/demographic groupings. A Jewish paper is instantly limited by circulation in America and so also a black paper. At one time it was only Ebony, a for-black American magazine, that broke even and showed profit, and even made the publisher, John H. Johnson, a billionaire.

(5) In Nigeria, despite the pretensions, the captive markets are essentially regional, that is ethnic or geopolitical. Take The Punch that will make a bestseller in the Lagos/South-West area, and does not make a dent in the East. So also Nigerian Tribune which has wide circulation in the West, but does not do particularly well in the North or East. Of course, the papers all fool their readers by the lie that Lagos and Abuja are Nigeria and that if one circulated well in those two cities one is by that national. It is a logic that simply fails on closer examination. The Abuja-Lagos inhabitants, who are non-indigenes, are economic migrants, even if only of the internal kind. And immigrants are often an active population segment, looking out for economic opportunities first and perhaps defined by that and not by their habitat. Though this may look like an overstatement, but at each critical time, it is proved over and over again. To give an example in the election of President Goodluck Jonathan, Igbo/South-Southerners in Lagos, Abuja, Kano, etc, voted like their counterparts in Enugu, Yenogoa, Oron, etc. That is, in matters of culture and major sensitivities, that is, for matters that are non-economic and outside monetary issues, their hearts are at home, and as one with the people they left behind. In the memorable phrase of the Igbo people, their hearts are at home even if their feet are abroad.

SOUTH-SOUTH SOCIOLOGY OF BUSINESS ADVANTAGES

Of all the indices that count, that are intrinsic to the entrepreneur - that is, gumption, vision and even cash - we can assume they are equally available to all Nigerians. The assumption is that we are all equally talented on the average across the ethnic divides, even if not as individuals. The individual discount has been made by the fact that these very successful men would have been successful anyway, in other fields, if the sociology does not specifically exclude them.

The critical position of the South-South is that they do not have any irrational viewpoints or obsessions to expound. They do not because they simply cannot. They are not being charitable. It is just that they cannot afford the resources and costs to author and finish the huge project of overwhelming the majorities, jointly or severally. Being a minority, that is, a people as powerless as can be, against ravaging, rampaging majorities, with their closing vice-like claws, the minority disadvantages are clear.

Unlike the majority power blocs of the North, the South-West and questionably, the South-East, who have achieved close to, or even critical mass, the South-South is way behind fissionable status. It is likely that any attempt by them to do so will be checked by any of their immediate great major/ power neighbours. This is besides the unlikely and rather insurmountable problem of the South-Southerners engineering a unity of voices and strategy across a region infamous for its diversity.

So this accident of being a minor, accords the South-South an operating and operational advantage, which no other zone has. Unlike the other zones, the South-South does not suffer a delusion of power, of one next move that will have us pacify the rest of Nigeria under our minority rule.

And even the majority-persons have found the task daunting. The nearest the majority came to it was the collusion between the North and the South-West which ran as fragilely as can be, till June 12, so-called, cracked the collusion irredeemably.

Being most powerless, the South-South's best bet incidentally, is in justice for all and in openness. Every back room deals will have them loose out in the long run.

Ultimately, the greater power centres, after exploiting them to achieve a specific grand aim, would all too likely discard them and move on to new engagements. This native fragility of collusion of the unequally yoked is illustrated by the South-West-North power grid, which ended in the political electric shock that was June 12. Professor Bolaji Akinyemi, who was dictator, Ibrahim Babangida's high prized surrogate and co-confederate of the very powers he is now blaming, found time to assert: "the present system is an imposition by a sectional elite that exploited its temporary occupation of the levers of power to seek an arrangement that would be an advantage to it. It is obvious to all that the centre can no longer hold (The Sun July 19, 2012)

On the fairground principle, the South-South has a secured ground. From Akinyemi's conclusion, it is evident that it is the North, who he and his South-West/Yoruba people served, even if as junior partners, that he refers to. However, what is not clearly stated is that the attempt by the North to impose, in Akinyemi's words, the present system is and has always been resisted by the other sectional elites, including his own South-West. The resistance may be undeclared, but a no less ferociously fought war has been going on.

Like we said earlier, the incapacity of the South-South to project power, ironically, is a source of power or what we may call the power of the impotent. Recall the power of palace eunuchs and extrapolate. Since the South-Southerners have not even started, they are not deluded like the other majority parties that, just one step, they are in perpetual power. They are therefore forced to mediate between warring contenders, who think power is just one strategic move away. As Akinyemi also acceded in the same paper, the elite are factionalised, and it is of course along geo-ethnic lines. So, while the big three are the legs of the tripod, the South-South are the rings that connect or brace them together, without which everything scatter scatter, Nigeria jaga jaga, gboza gboza!

Clearly, connecting and connections are all the media do. Indeed, there may be no greater connective and bracing tissue in the world than the media. The power of connection, of the brace, actually resides in the hands of the non-belligerents that are independent. So the South-South wins.

On the project of not antagonising the ruling class that already is antagonised within itself, the factionalised parties, that is the majority ethnic's best bet is, if they are to be believed, individually, to go to a South-South media.

It would have been an insult or an invitation to war if a Northerner/Easterner/Westerner decides to issue a decree and gave it to a fellow Northerner, or Easterner or Westerner to announce. He needs to co-opt a third party, who apparently is innocent. The best party to deliver a sucker punch is a man who can be assumed innocent. If the punch is against his people, the third party agent is finished. To give an example, Senator Bola Tinubu, who is practically the Yoruba leader on the political turf, has always suggested that Obasanjo, who, in the several instances he was used as an innocent third party by the North, sold the Yoruba into slavery (The Punch, April 25, 2010)

Luckily, Obasanjo has openly confessed in The Punch (August 27, 2011) interview that he knew nothing of the Murtala Mohammed coup for which the Northerners hired him as an innocent third party and second in command, to his junior, and overrated General Murtala Mohammed. This situation of being a northern hireling has since rendered Obasanjo a poor electoral asset in his South-West region. Any unpopular politician or party cannot own or mount a podium or a platform and sell well his person, any message. In fact, his person and associated or potential assets are rejected a priori. This will always be the fate of a majority third party agent to another majority party. That is, majority-agent third parties and their platforms or media cannot be bestsellers in their home region. Simply put, media floated by an Obasanjo are a priori non-bankable asset.

On the captive market, the South-Southerners are not as down as they may seem at first glance. Truth is that they lack the home population, making only about 12% of the population. However, those who have it, the North the South-West and South-East are all in the race to appear as nationalists on the face of contrived facts. But in truth they are all and individually gunning for their private and regional agenda if not hegemony. So they all have a self-defeating and self-cancelling platform and programme. This is best measured by the fact that no Nigerian leader comes nearly being a national icon. We are all divided not just by our nationalities but also by our matching sub-nations. Our most famous heroes Awolowo, Azikiwe/Ojukwu and Bello/Murtala are all trapped into their regional cocoons as heroes. Not one of them crosses borders and is taken as a nationalist. And to worsen matters, all other Nigerian heroes have followed faithfully the same path. Obasanjo is Ogboni, Ekwueme is Ofo, Shagari is Arewa, and Clark is Egbesu, etc. Ogboni, Ofo, Arewa and Egbesu are iconic symbols of our Yoruba, Igbo, Hausa-Fulani and Ijaw nationalities respectively.

Decidedly, no major paper has chosen to be or declare itself regional. The apparent part of the explanation is that the economics of advertising, (a consequence it is worthy to remark, of the two Security Council, North Hausa/Fulani and South-West, Yoruba arrangement of Nigeria) would not suggest it. However, we suspect that if we can overcome our constitutive fears, a newspaper can be sustained avowedly on regional interests and circulation alone. However, this tragedy of Nigeria built to mean little other than Lagos and Abuja portends greater dangers than we are willing to know. First of all, it is a lie that we are nationalists because we inhabit Abuja and Lagos. And secondly, it supports and encourages unitarism in media and other spheres, which is all what we are arms against. Perhaps, another essay will only do full justice to this.

Since the majority powers all want to be really regional, and while pretending to be nationalists just to appear politically correct, the nearest people to a national and nationalist group are the South-Southerners. This is by the logic and irony of being powerless and a highly vulnerable group but not out of their innate goodness. That is, their very survival is in keeping in the open all that goes on. Openness and transparency are the best bet for any endangered peoples. And here again the minorities of the South-South wins, and this shows up in their media prowess concomitantly.

THE FUTURE

Since the warring big three are not willing or able to resolve their issues, (the constitution review panel being a circus), the configuration of sociology and power will remain the same and the South-South will trump all others in the media business, for a long time to come. Except the power balance is radically changed as to go regional, the power of this minority moguls will remain unchallenged, and substantially unchallengeable. Their sociology of advantage is unrivalled and nothing will likely alter it in the short and medium terms. In the long run, we all are, of course, dead. So, why bother with a non-bankable the long term.

It is not just that the South-South dominates as fact, they should in logic. All sociology of business advantage, the mother of all advantages, is on their side. It is only normal in business that they will out-game and beat the others in the race. And we are in a democracy and the media is an open market business. It is unlike the Nigerian oil industry which is so regulated, anti-market, and anti-competitively operated. And it shows, as all oil industry conferences and exhibitions since 1970 have studiedly been held in Lagos and Abuja. It is anti-nature, and it is anti-competition to talk of the sea in a desert tent. It is like holding oil exhibition in America in Washington and not in Houston. It tells that something is wrong. It tells that bureaucrats, politicians, rigged national constitution by a tribal military faction, apologies to Akinyemi, and that a critical part of Nigerian endowment, oil, is run as a mafia possession. And when they do, corruption is the rule.

To conclude on this section, the civil war in media terms may have paid the minorities the greatest dividends. Lest we forget, it costs them quite a lot, the least of which is the confiscation and robbery of their natural resource, crude oil. This, too, is beyond the scope of this paper.

SOUTH-SOUTH SOCIOLOGY OF BUSINESS ADVANTAGES

The race to have a balanced newspaper reflecting all opinions: The Guardian studiedly started it even as it had Yoruba-core dominance. That is, her opinion pages were apparently open to persons/intellectuals from various geopolitical zones at any one time, plausibly as a deliberate attempt. This was, of course, different from New Nigerian or Daily Times of the old which made a fetish of what gods they were serving. Apparently for the Ibrus, all that mattered was that The Guardian sold and that no section/party's partisan view point be singly or singularly canvassed. This was, we repeat, to the interest of the Ibrus, as businessmen and South-South persons and minority power contenders. Their greatest moment will only come when the majority tribes are in contention with one another, and not in collusive agreement. The minorities would have their opening and can trade on these shifting lines of majority discord. That was the basis of the survival of most third world regimes during the Soviet-U.S. cold war. After the fall of the Soviet Union, America and her allies just went in and busted Iraq and Libya. In the days of the cold war, Libya and Iraq would have run to the Soviets and their dictators would have survived. What is now lengthening the days of the Syrian dictator is the new coming to things of China and an awakened Russia. If the majorities ever came together or to real peace and harmony, they will crush all the minority powers, including Syria, into dust.

Now Vanguard has nudged up the ante. While The Guardian took to ostensibly pan-Nigerian writers who had their peculiarities or obsessions edited away, Vanguard has two Northern writers in a South-South/Southern paper. The critical difference here is that these people are allowed to write as they would have written for New Nigerian, that is virulently anti-South and crassly pro-North pieces. It might be of some interest that the Yoruba owned paper, The Nation, that allowed or copied this format did so only at a time it was run by a South-Southerner, Mr. Victor Ifijeh, as Managing Director/Editor-in-Chief. He hired a pro-North, Northern writer, Haruna Mohammed and gave him, unedited, a South-West-owned media platform. To give a full flavour of what we are saying let us quote how a leading Southwest intellectual characterised Haruna Mohammed: "Snooper is aware that in many enlightened and influential circles particularly in the South-West of the nation, Mohammed Haruna is viewed with political anxiety, to put things diplomatically. Not a few are often affronted by and aghast at what they consider his rightwing reactionary worldview, his overt and covert gaming for northern interests at the expense of national interest, the impish sangfroid with which he puts his views across and the devastating clarity of his presentation.... There are those who think that Mohammed Haruna's fierce rallying to a pan-Islamic front is a backhanded glorification of the rigidly patriarchal and feudal authoritarian code and a tacit endorsement of the spiritual enslavement and religious colonisation of others such as we have seen in many variants of Islam (The Nation July 22, 2012- Snooper, as everyone who should know, is a ranking professor of South-West extraction. Some even allege he is Professor Adebayo Williams. But we are not in sufficient authority to confirm or deny this)

There is no doubt that the views of Snooper columnist are the ruling views in Yoruba land. It simply follows that were The Nation entirely a Yoruba run and owned paper, and if as we learnt, Ifijeh did not extract the promise to be given free managerial hands, that a Mohammed would not have been or lasted as a columnist with a mainstream Yoruba media vehicle. Originally, The Nation was a certain paper named the Comet, which wobbled commercially. Ifijeh, the South-Southerner was hired and brought in as a turnaround expert.

There is little doubt that the minority instinct to reach out started as mere instinct. But now, as is often the case, it is morphing into an attitude, into a skill and may be later, into a formalised thinking or strategy. It is the duty of scholars and watchers to be ahead of the curve and help the actors see the end of the road, even before they have put on their boots to embark or gone far.

These minority people are able to do this because theirs is not to go for a cause, they in themselves can't have or project any partisan course. It is in their best interest to have a fair federation by default. Otherwise, being the weakest, they are the most disposable, and they know it, or should.

It must be noted that this feat of a virulently anti-North, Southern writer cannot be accommodated in a Northern paper that comes with an agenda, at least not in Daily Trust and Leadership newspapers as they come today. It will be the equivalent of a Reagan allowing Gorbachev to open an FM Radio or TV station in New York. No big power or region with power of deluded grandeur or its own exceptionalisms or high destiny, does that. The implication is that the viewpoint of those with a sense of high destiny sells lower in the market place. So to sell best they need a dictatorship or its moral equivalent to secure their markets. This accounts for the cultural hyper-sensitivities of closed dictatorial systems, whether it is Saudi Arabia, North Korea or parts of northern Nigeria.

Finally, let us observe on this sub-heading the fact that there are investment and dividend implications in promoting or investing in a South-South-owned and or directed media against a majority counterpart. That is to say, this study has practical implication as much as a formal business spreadsheet.

And we can confess that we have used the sociology of business advantage template repeatedly to predict the fate of new enterprises and have also used the political market equivalent to predict political careers almost too presciently for our belief. It is a new model but it works as much if not better in certain circumstances than the old one.

PRACTISING INNOCENCE

One of the earliest media experiences etched into my mind was at a conference and Goodie Ibru made a comment and I quote from memory; that as a media owner himself (he is part of the Ibru family majority share-owning promoters of The Guardian) and a friend of another media owner, Chief Emmanuel Iwuanyanwu, he understood that a publisher is not often dictating to his journalists. So when Champion, Iwuanyanwu's paper, writes stories that are not flattering to him, he knows Iwuanyanwu has no hand in it, despite the promptings to the contrary by other friends. Of course, people complain to him that The Guardian rubbishes them but perhaps they would not understand he is not dictating or suggesting they do.

As true as this is, the unfortunate thing is that nobody believes it. This will be especially so if you have an agendum or are suspected of having one. Thus if you are thought of having an agendum before you and the media you own or run are arraigned for trial you are already deemed guilty.

The example of a piece written by Sam Omatseye, of The Nation will illustrate this. In his column in The Nation allegedly owned by Bola Tinubu, he wrote a neither too charitable, nor a too damnable piece on the Awolowo brood. And all hell was let loose.

But like in all such quarrel, the real issues were not mentioned as everybody skirted around them. For the Awolowos, a powerful political Yoruba clan, the real issue is that Tinubu was the author and finisher of that essay and little would it matter under what by-line it was carried. The reasons are as follows; the Awolowos and the Tinubu factions are in undeclared, shadow and proxy wars. The matter is over who inherits or annexes the now dead patriarch, Awolowo's considerable political and inspirational legacy. Already Tinubu is, some would say, the pre-emptively-styled Asiwaju, a Yoruba honorific for the leader, possibly of the race. And he apparently achieved this, by one account, without the active blessing of or acknowledging the seigniorage of the Awolowo brood or political clan. And it appears the Awolowos and their sympathizers are not too readily disposed to Tinubu being a Yoruba leader, presumptive, or otherwise.

Within this environment and setting Tinubu was not only a suspect, he needed to prove himself innocent, otherwise he will be considered guilty, a political criminal. And all too probably he was a marked man, as himself was thought of as an assassin or capable of hiring one, in political terms anyway.

So, for the Awolowos, a paper owned by Tinubu, a contender and political enemy or non-ally, is also an enemy armament, and paper massed against you. It therefore follows that its cognate columns and every comma must be studied. Also, all its gestures even those of, or that are statements of goodwill, will be checked for hidden motives or verbal or landmines. It has to be read and divined as cold war Washington power players did the Pravda's (of USSR) every comma. Even a comma, misplaced, can trigger a Soviet-U.S. confrontation, as a Henry Kissinger will tell. The two powers tried to contain the opportunity for damage by opening a hotline between the White House and Kremlin. But between the Tinubu and an Awolowo factions there are no such formal safety valve arrangements.

The point of all this is that if Omatseye was writing in a paper without political agenda, or suspected political agenda, as majority power papers often do, then the matter would have at its worse been resolved over telephone calls. And the fact that Omatseye wrote it will now be believed. Otherwise, for the Awolowos, Tinubu is and remains the author.

Now, it will be important to remark that Tinubu's answer is the usual canned retort by publishers that they do not interfere. That is only true if you are discussing football and there are no life and death issues at stake. If there are, then the suspicions are so much that all that matter is perception, not the reality. In fact, the perception becomes or is acted upon to become the reality.

It is not important that the accusation or assumptions that Tinubu ordered Omatseye to write an anti-Awo piece are true. What is important is that the accusations are believed, and that this belief is the basis of the actions and reactions of the parties. America went to war against Iraq because it believed that the Iraqis had weapons of mass destruction. When after the war no weapons of mass destruction were found, other reasons had to be invented to rationalise the war. The point is that the West believed itself against an enemy, Sadaam Hussein and his country, Iraq. The issue, we repeat, is perception, not reality. Anyway perception and not reality is what the written world is all about, including the broadsheets and newspapers like The Nation.

This is also one of the reasons those who owned media houses in Nigeria have never quite made it to the presidency. They can make it to the region, but to the presidency, babu. And to be fair to the dictator Ibrahim Babangida, he annulled presumptive president MKO Abiola's election, in part, on the weight of the enemies Abiola made on the business of owning and running National Concord. Earlier, the same money bag was told the presidency was not for the highest bidder, which should really be read to mean the loudest (media) mouth. Politically, it is a risky investment to own media channels. Already, people are mythologizing it, that it is a divine or some mysterious curse to own a media or to pre-announce your presidential ambitions. It is all a similar sociology at work and play, and there are ways about and around it. But we shall attend to those in another paper. In fact, to sort of pre-empt our paper the South-South can use their media assets as a studied political dividend and not just entrepreneurial asset.

ELECTRONIC MEDIA

On May 20, 2012, about 8pm Deji Badmos hosted his programme Politics Today on Channels TV. His guests were rather unusual. They were proxy gladiators of sorts. Dr. Doyin Okupe came in for the Peoples Democratic Party, and Lai Mohammed was there for his Action Congress of Nigeria and a phone in guest, Famakin was on phone from Abuja for Congress for Progressive Change.

It was unusual in that this was the first time I saw gladiators verbally punch themselves at Deji's show. It is usually peopled by so-called civil society types and they are often on one, even if blurred page.

The second oddity is that there are other television stations like TVC, allegedly or believably owned by Tinubu and NTA owned by the Federal Government but controlled by the ruling party, practically.

But it is simply unimaginable that these three men would have gathered under the cover of TVC or NTA. And this situation, we should remark, would have remained even if Deji jumped ship and anchors for TVC/NTA.

That is, Deji's ability to bring in big names, separated into partisan camps, has little to do with his professional competence, integrity or lack of it. Deji's strength is in the perceived neutrality of the Channels TV medium. One fact that needs repeating is that Channels TV can get its most power and prestige and glory in and by being neutral or perceived neutral. As a minority, Channels TV's best habitat is in neutrality. Firstly, unlike the TVC, Channels TV does not have a captive large market to sustain itself as a non-market competition driven vehicle. TVC can live and thrive as a for-Yoruba only TV channel. Partisanship pays her in the short term, but not Channels TV. This must be understood. That is, Channels TV people, or better still, the minority peoples, are not necessarily or by nature nicer human beings. They are forced to be. There is no good man. And Jesus says so, too, "Why do you call me good? Nobody is good except God".

Perhaps, this proves the assertion that the medium is the message. If the medium is pre-assumed innocent, (it need not be, it is perception that matters) the clans, however, broken into factions, will gather about her marquee to share communion in words or wine. That is, it is simply unlikely for Okupe to appear under a TVC programme hosted by Deji, and share turf with Lai Mohammed.

Presently, TVC has headhunted or poached Deji-style professionals, but these professionals, even while good at their job, are tainted by the reflected Tinubu visage, as backdrop. The point, we repeat, is not whether they are tainted. It is just that they are seen as tainted and that shapes the reactions and reception people give to her truths and programmes. That is, all TVC, read a majority-owned and ran media, suffers an agenda discount. And in an open market this will lower their market share and worsen their capacity to attract top talent.

Already, a well conceived programme Fireworks, hosted on TVC by a South-Southerner anchor is rested. It has not been aired in a couple of months or thereabout. And to worsen matters, a programme that should be attracting national audience, today attracts only South-West guests. It is so region-bound, by default, not design, we have to plausibly concede that it has gone so low, as to have local government guest-contenders. Simply put, no PDP persons will trust TVC. The suspicion is that TVC has and harbours a loaded, even secret agenda or microphone. And major powers must by nature be partisan.

In the end, they, the majority and minority power contenders, will all run to the Channels TV, AITs and Silverbirds of this world to find voice and, even more importantly, to be believed. There is a majority discount on the news that NTA and TVC all suffer that would not afflict the Channels TV, AITs and Silverbirds of this world, since they apparently have little to gain by telling lies to favour the dominant majority parties. The key word is apparently, that is, perception is simultaneously the turf, the game and the goal. And again it all plays out to the favour and even flavour of being a minority.

LANGUAGE AT WORK AND PLAY

All the while we have not talked about language, which itself is the medium that carries the content. Like all media, language is the message, but this will be largely unknown to many, including some practitioners till it is dedicatedly investigated.

Of course, big name writers like Professor Wole Soyinka will know. For a Soyinka, just where to put, or not put a comma, can give him migraine headaches an Emzor Paracetamol may never cure. Why because he knows it can make the difference between thunder and a whimper.

We will give one example. When Colonel Sambo Dasuki was appointed as security adviser to President Jonathan, The Punch in an accompanying piece characterised former dictator Ibrahim Babangida as a despot. Well, Babangida is. But so also are former dictators like Yakubu Gowon, Muhammadu Buhari, Abdulsalami Abubakar, Olusegun Obasanjo, and Murtala Mohammed. Babangida's singular sin, which is now a privatised obsession between the South-West and the North/Babangida, is his North's annulment of an election allegedly won by Chief M.K.O. Abiola. Chief M.K.O. Abiola, like the promoters of The Punch, is Yoruba and comes from the South-West zone. And I have never read any writer in The Punch call the others despots. So an unseen prejudice creeps in, altering perceptions now and later. Yet The Punch writer, in making his choice of words, would not likely be aware he is making an exceptional case of Babangida, that he is fighting the regional war, even if armed with only his typewriter and his reporter's notebooks. Anyway, it is on record Babangida could not have been Nigeria's worst despot. The very dubious honour goes to General Yakubu Jack Gowon, who is one of Africa's top ten genocidists. But since a mass murderer didn't kill one Yoruba man, he is counted a nationalist or even a saint. Other people, in spite of themselves, are hell. One could exterminate them, with lovely conscience, and Gowon did and is approved of by the South-West/Yoruba.

What it means is that although we share one space we suffer multiple worldviews about a critical time, and are other peoples to one another. Our frame and scales of references are often different and full of interferences that are group-specific and may be self-cancelling or incomprehensible across groups. And tragically it shows; our choice of heroes separates us. And they, our heroes, do not cross ethnic borders. Nigeria has no national heroes. What we have is a collage, a composite of heroes, of and for the various nationalities. It is this compositeness of heroes in a forced unitary mould that is best habitat for minority genius.

Perhaps, it has to be understood that the America never planned to be a superpower. It saw a vacuum or met the facts on the ground, and took up the default choice of being a superpower. The fact on the ground was that Europe was comatose. So the major tribes or powers are just not all warlike. It is that there is a visible fact on the ground or vacuum for power. And each one of the major blocs appears to be one step away to super majority. But it is the same optical illusion that brought Napoleon and Hitler and the Europe of their times to ruins. It never quite gets to work. The last time the North tried it with June 12, we have not all resolved it. And when Nzeogwu made the coup the North interpreted it as a bid for Igbo dominance, and it led directly to one of the signal genocides in Africa, thanks to General Yakubu Gowon.

CONCLUSION

With nearly all the sociology of business advantage, which by the way, is the mother of all advantages on the credit and favour of the South-South, it will amount to the worst form of intellectual irresponsibility and or unpardonable ignorance to still hold that the South-South are in conspiracy to own the media or the banks or are able to do so only because of revenue windfalls from oil, as the Arewa Consultative Forum in, say, Vanguard, September 29, 2012 in a piece by its official voice, Mr. Anthony Sanni: These days, those who are beating are the ones who are crying. How do you justify the fact that most of the banks are owned by the people from the South-South? How do you justify the situation where most of the media houses are owned by people from the South-South? You think that they are the hardest workers?

And if we are to follow up, are the South-Southerners the people who have the most money, or more stolen money than all others? Whoever stole more power or money than Nigeria's military despots? Is any one of those a South-Southerner? It is just that the sociology of business makes the South-South to dominate in these market sectors. And whom nature and events bless should not stand accused for their success, which is no crime of theirs. It is like accusing Kenyans, who dominate the world long distance and marathon races, of having been born into a hilly country side. Or even back home, to accuse the Yoruba for the crime of bearing more twins, or if you liked princes, than the rest of Nigeria pulled together. Wisdom is in recognising nature and living in harmony with her. God or nature has granted each, majority and minority, her own blessings.

Perhaps, the question we should be asking is, why are the Northern minorities not harvesting the same sociology of business dividends if it is a minority share bonus? I can assure the sociology explains it still. Even though the northern minorities are not too off the mark it is just that they have not achieved dominance due to them. And we will pay attention to this on a later paper. Apparently, because sociology of business analysis is a fairly new area, there are too many openings and investigations and papers yet to be written on it.

Let us rest the matter on Achebe. We have no quarrel with Ulu.... But I will not see with these eyes of mine his priest making himself lord over us. My father... did not tell me that Ezeulu was king in Umuaro. Who is he, anyway? Does anybody here enter his compound through the man's gate? If Umuaro decided to have a king we know where he would come from. Since when did Umuachala become the head of the six villages? We all know that it was jealousy among the big villages that made them give the priesthood to the weakest. (Arrow of God by Chinua Achebe)

The minorities are the Umuachalas, the weakest among us. They shall remain our priests; that is, the near monopoly vectors that bind us together, save our jealousy becomes history. And even then, it may have been just too late, with the threshold, the Rubicon, already crossed.

It is additionally instructive it is the priesthood that they (Umuachalas) were given. That is, they had a monopoly on administering religion. And we can ably recall that the word 'religion' itself, as has been held by many sociologists, including Joseph Campbell and George Grant, who write that religion... arises most likely from the Latin "to bind together". Religion and the State, from Technology and Empire By George Grant (House of Anansi, 1969). That is, in other words, to brace together, to supply the connectives that make us an integrated whole, to make us a self-subsisting organism. And it gets more interesting, as Grant writes further, and correctly we hold: "That is, as that system of belief (whether true or false) which binds together the life of individuals and gives to those lives whatever consistency of purpose they may have." And gives to those lives whatever consistency of purpose (or dynamism, as we shall canvass and prefer) they may have.

This religious or bracing role of the minorities in variant and competitive universes stretches beyond them and is important in those universes as the universes' sustainers and stabilizers. Minorities are also able to act as key prompters and propellants for the progress of their universes. We cannot quite bond or prosper without our minorities.

The thesis is that the minorities may need to come to knowledge and charge appropriate premiums for this sociology of transactions and relationships monopoly. It is a minority media century in Nigeria and beyond, or would you not think so?

2

How And Why
The Warri Dons Dominate
The Comedy Business

Now everybody who should knows the Waffians (or folks from Warri) dominate the multi-million comedy business in Nigeria. Waffians is, of course, the nickname these Warri boys go by. Now, are there any reasons on earth the Waffian should dominate this comedy trade? Is it genetic? No. An accident... perhaps... but not.... Sociology of market forces? And we did say, yes!

Here is a psycho-graph of the "Warri nation" and the characteristics that predispose them towards their existential options and choices: Warri is the oil city of Delta State. That is to say, it is the hub town for the populace that services the oil industry, scattered all over the Greater Warri. And their petro-dollar lifestyle is appropriately opulent.

And Warri is Nigeria's only and truly pot-pourri city. More than Lagos or any other Nigerian town, Warri has the curse or blessing of not having any aboriginal population of any critical size. Even if you granted the Isekiri, the Ijaw or even the Urhobo each, aboriginality, the population quotient each contributes to Warri viz a viz themselves and all others (Nigerians and foreigners) is not significant in numbers or cultural terms. This is especially important, because despite the cant of certain population mavens, Warri is more cosmopolitan than Lagos. Why do we say so? Lagos has a captive aboriginal population of "Lagosians" so-called. But Lagosians are a subset of the Yoruba nation. The trooping in of the other Yoruba into Lagos, joins as one with the native Lagosians, to form a very significant and absorbent mother population of the Yoruba.

Thus while Lagos carries a larger variety of national groups, the significance of the native population is still overwhelming... giving Lagos a dominant, even if corrupted, Yoruba culture.

In Warri there is no such mother culture and all cultures, both immigrant and aboriginal, contend with one another, with no favoured competitors. This is critical as we shall see later. The next critical feature of Warri is that it was, and still, is a town of minorities... of the alienated. Minorities first in the Nigerian sense of and against majority tribes, and also of an impoverished native population living side by side with the opulence of European oil workers, their local retainers and or enforcers.

Bewildered and schizophrenic, the Waffians were left on their own. To worsen matters, their women, like the women of all tribes and tongues, were the first to cross boundary into the hands of the new conquerors; that is, the European oil workers and their coterie.

The results are evident. The larger Warri, perhaps, boasts of more mulatto population than the rest of Nigeria put together. This European contact may have given the Waffians an (imitative?) sophistication and individuality, aligned to an irreverence, which is not quite found anywhere else – not even among the very republican Igbo.

This further fuelled a dichotomy and the creation of what we may call Town Waffians and street Waffians. (This after the town and cattle Fulani parallel).

Among the town Warrians (not really Waffians any more) you find entrenched commercial ruling houses who pretend or are actually trading on timber, fish, estates, etc, but actually own vast and endless estates and tracks of land all over the Greater Warri. They constitute a Fulani-style aristocracy, but without a religious doctrine to push it. So, apparently they rely on licences, and collusive contacts and contracts with governments to suggest privilegensia and its studied transference to their children. While Igbo, for instance, have more (anonymous) rich men, the Greater Warri plutocrats, are nationally well branded with dynasties to match.

This left the Warri poor to themselves, and the question was what to do? If we count on the insights of the Spanish sociologist, Ortega Gasset, civility is a tool to ease the pain and difficulties of relationships, of communications. We are thus civil to our neighbours because we do not want to bump into one another.

And we are humorous because we wish to be able to bear our limitations, our interactions, as underlings and attendant harsh environments, with as much good cheer as can. It is a social tool of survival, without which many races and individuals would have perished.

And if we are to believe the British academic, Des MacHale, one of the finest authorities on witticism and humour, the two wittiest races are the Jews and the Irish.

Of the two, the Jews, like the Waffians, are some of the most cosmopolitan peoples (in the earlier sense of Warri not Lagos). And alas, the Waffians have also suffered the most, apparently without any big brothers to want to rescue them.

Many know of the Jewish pogroms, but equally appalling are the humiliation and death in millions that Britain procured upon the Irish by official incompetence and mismanagement. This led to potato famine, which in part pushed the Irish to join the exodus train to America... and the rest is history. Of course, great humour, like its equivalent in love affairs and lyrics, is in the inheritance of the doomed and the sorrowful. All (literary) history confirms this.

Thus for the Jews and the Irish to survive they needed humour... and have for all you know produced the greater numbers... and possibly the world's best in Oscar Wilde and Woody Allen. Thus comedy is a tool and a stance against humiliation and where one is suddenly able to laugh at oneself and laugh away ill-luck, minority induced-humiliation, and stay alive. And as Jean-Dominique Bauby, a former Editor of French Elle, and a massive stroke victim educates us, with The Divinity-Bell, his world famous memoir, There comes a time when the heaping-up of calamities brings on uncontrollable nervous laughter-when, after a final blow from fate, we decide to treat it all as a joke.

It is important we appreciate it is not something genetic. We are dealing with sociology and history. And as the British philosopher Whitehead Alfred reminds us, the total absence of humour from the Bible is one of the most singular things in all literature. That is to say, the Jews acquired their "genius" for humour, post the Bible (written by the Jews, essentially) era. So the question is why?

Our postulation is that to be in humour and possess a genius for humour or comedy, you need to be largely devoid of hope. But the Jews were not. Prior to the Bible, they believed in the coming of a messiah; that is, they had hope. Hope slipped off their palms, as a series of pogroms dogged them all over Europe, which they considered or thought as sanctuary. By the time of Hitler, they had lost all hope of a coming messiah and took their destiny and safety unto their hands, in part, with humour.

So, as we can see the Waffians have all the attributes that lead to the "industrial" production of humour as a staple for survival.

1. They are a minority, largely devoid of the redeeming power of hope

2. They, as a pot-pourri of contending minorities, had to devise tools of harmony and civilised behaviour. And humour has through history been one way to actually tell a guy to go to hell and he would actually look forward to the journey; that is; being diplomatic; even if irreverent.

3. The Town Warris treated them, the Waffians, like stray dogs, thus binding together, in a critical and creative

intercourse that is not available in any other Nigerian settlement except possibly, Ajegunle. Across international borders other similar towns are Trench Town, Jamaica and Harlem, the U.S.. And they are justly famous; for Ajegunle, creative football, music; Jamaica, reggae and sports (cricket, track and field), Warri, besides humour, a patio that is one of the sweetest talk ever brewed by man; Harlem, jazz, sports (basket ball).

The import is that the Waffians are likely to produce the greatest numbers and best in that field, especially at the top end of the market. And this is not just in per capital terms, but in absolute numbers despite their being a minority people. So, could there be other reasons why the Waffians dominate the national comedy trade, since they are a minority people?

More than their skills, their minority status also plays a critical role. Doubt that, then listen to this. I once ran into an Igbo comedian and he told a private joke. I asked why he would not go national with it. He said the Yoruba, on hearing it, will hunt and run him out of town and market.

And what was the joke? He said that in after-life the Heads of State and Prime Ministers of Singapore, South Korea, Taiwan, and Nigeria held a closed door meeting with God. God was bitter with Sir Abubakar Tafawa Balewa on how Nigeria turned up a mess. Sir Balewa smiled and answered God, give anyone of those countries, just a handful of Yoruba men, and let us see if that country would not be made ungovernable. And it was said God understood and acquitted Balewa.

I quite understood, too. If a South Easterner or Northerner spoke such to the Yoruba, it could cause an OPC-MASSOB and or OPC-Boko Haram war. But a minority people without any imperial ambitions or capacities, can get away with such expensive jokes. And they saw, perhaps instinctively, this advantage and made a career of yabbis, a Nigerian lingo for abrasive jokes, on the three big nations of Igbo, Hausa-Fulani and Yoruba.

As we write many will remind us that now there are Igbo, Yoruba and Hausa comedy artistes yabbing theirs and other others' ethnic nations. Yes. But that is only now that comedy has matured or is about to, as an independent and self-subsisting industry. In the beginning, only the minorities could do it and go free. We must also remind ourselves that at a point the State Security Service (SSS) (now Department of State Services - DSS) surreptitiously muscled in to stop any further anti-President Obasanjo public jokes or yabbis. So, things are not always as harmless as they seem.

Even more a minority humorist must not make an anti-Warri joke to balance up an anti-Igbo or Yoruba or Hausa joke. He has the creative freedom, blank cheque, to be as free roaming as he can be. But for an Igbo humorist to get it right with an anti-Yoruba or anti-Hausa comic quip, he must have a repertoire of anti-Igbo jokes, or be thought anti other nationals. And that is, he is foreclosing on his market as a man who eats because he talks to make others laugh. This handicap does not exist for the minority humour merchant.

It was this head start, to give it to the oppressor nations of Igbo, Yoruba and Hausa, that so endeared the minorities to the comedy box office. And as one success followed another, all Warri comedy wannabes are now abandoning Warri for the big stage in the Abuja-Lagos axis, where the big box offices are and happen.

Thus it is this history-cum-sociology induced talent for humour and irreverence, plus a population tripod stand, upon which they are a connecting or brace ring, which has ensured comedy business will be made by Waffians for a long time to come.

And being minorities, only they would have had the third eye to see in a most penetrative and bewitching innocence, the faults and foibles of the big tribes, who by sheer number, constitute the greater market.

3

Why And How
The Golden Deltans Dominate
Nigerian Banking

Mallam F. Bello is the Chief Executive of Unity Bank. He once went to town with the retort that the South East and the Delta State players among themselves control or own 60 per cent and more of the Nigerian banking assets. He might as well have been right, save that he showed tragic mischief or ignorance or possibly both, on the "geography" of banking assets, ownership, control or power. Of course, his was a glancing sort of blow against Professor Chukwuma Soludo, the then CBN Governor. Bello's unhidden take is that Soludo consolidated Nigerian banks into the hands of the Igbo and their Delta State cousins. A terrible charge sheet of conspiracy and other crimes, one would say.

However, a detailed look at the available data will reveal the following. That Bello was playing at a Nazi-style category game. That is, geography, geopolity and ethnicity are shaped, reshaped or altered to serve a priori conclusions. Like Herman Goering, a great Nazi bureaucrat ('I determine who is a Jew!'), Bello's paranoia was on alleged Igbo (Jewish for Goering) domination of the Nigerian (world for the Jewish) financial landscape, where actually there is none. It might be fit to remark that because of this false charge, "a few million" Jews, in part, were gassed to death.

Secondly, of the banks in question, the South East players only control or own the middle size banks, a la Diamond, Fidelity, Fin Bank. These banks together or playing alone

47

would have no real consequential muscle as to be considered bell weathers or market makers.

The truth of the matter is that Delta State, and more generally the South-South minorities (a non-member state of the South East geopolity and loose economic community) controls, runs or owns a disproportionate share of the Nigerian banking assets. This is given, and incontestable.

Our thesis, however, is that this is not a result of any conspiracies, but a consequence of known and determinable vectors that help shape and fashion market dynamics. Or, one can justifiably say that what is going on is what we may call the sociology of markets in action. And it plays out in markets as far apart as Tokyo, New York or Lagos. It is a pity we are paying no studied consideration of this phenomenon in the much of the world's markets, and especially the Nigerian variant. But we shall with this effort begin to make amends. Of course, we hope there will be no gassing of The Jews or just about anybodies here. Ignorance can breed so much evil!

Now the truth is, among themselves the Golden bankers (please remember the Golden Greeks of the merchant vessels fame) from the Big Delta, that is the South-South minorities, control the big name and biggest banks - UBA, Afribank, Zenith and Oceanic. One can tally in Union Bank on the larger Delta plank. And of the hot-shop banks, that is the small to medium size banks, which could shape tomorrow with new vistas, these Delta Golden boys again have near total dominance. From Bank PHB, a broad-spectrum fast maturing financial bull, to Access, a polo sponsoring high-street wannabe, to BGL, a template financial young Turk and Stanbic-IBTC with the retiring Atedo Peterside still around, it is clear Nigerian banking is substantially made in Big Delta terms. Of course, if one factored in Ms Evelyn Oputu of the Bank of Industry, the picture becomes sharper and intimidating.

So, how did this happen and why? Before we go further, let us recall a certain incident in our recent history. Many moons ago, Dr. Achike Udenwa, then the Governor of Imo

State, visited Lagos, and made a ward-round of the banks. His itinerary was to the South East bankers (CEOs) and their Big Delta states or South-South minorities counterparts, including Oceanic, (where I was part of the dedicated press related team). It so happened he did not or could not make it to "regional banks" controlled by the South Westerners or the Northerners.

Subsequently and acting, we believe on his own, a certain South-West Governor visited Lagos. He also made the same banking ward rounds. His itinerary avoided South East "regional" banks, but visited those of the South West and the Big Deltans. Also, a certain Northern Governor came to town and his preference was for the Golden boys and sometimes "gals" from the Big Delta.

What this portends is that in the universe of Nigerian banking, the Big Deltans constitute a subset of services□ suppliers on demand nationwide, suffering no market prejudice from any subset financial services consumer. This is a state of affairs no other geopolitical providers can claim to its credit. Or to put it more graphically, the three compounded geopolitical zones, aka the Hausa-Fulani, the Igbo and the Yoruba, each has a locked-in preference and trust for the Big Deltan or South-South minority bankers, alongside or even before their own indigenous players.

Immediately this fact and factor is absorbed, the question to ask is, why. Is it a Delta-driven conspiracy? No. Is it something in their genes? No. Their culture? No. What then is it? It is simply a sociology of the Nigerian existence (and thus markets) that plays in their financial favour. The truth that drives this is sometimes not spoken but is there. It is that these three hegemons or geopolities, aka Hausa-Fulani, Igbo, Yoruba, are jostling for power, influence and dominance. And like the brilliant Harvard scholar, Professor Nail Ferguson remarked, Hegemony is equal to Hege-money.

Thus if you denied your opponent or competitor his finances or financial strength, it will weaken his imperial outreach, and strategic flanks. It is thus in the geopolitical (sociology) interest of the contending powers of the East, the West and North to, as subtly as they can, take money out of the reach of fellow contenders, or seize it themselves, (which could lead to open declaration of war), or better still, put it in the hands of political neutrals. This state of existential and or political neutrality is what the Big Deltans or minority clan bankers have, if not achieved, successfully projected. Thus Delta is our financial Switzerland. As for the bankers from the compounded geopolitical zones of the East, the West and North, they are like Orwellian saints, guilty first until proven innocent.

This existential trading or sociology of market capital alone will out-weigh all others, not excluding balance sheet size, operating skills. In fact and ironically, because of it, both top talents and increasing customs will gravitate to her. This alone ensures these Big Deltans will stand above all other banker competitors, as Switzerland and London do in the world's financial markets.

If we took the matter to other lands, the same experiences duplicate themselves. City of London, for instance, is the world's premier capital for international finance. She out-competes Wall Street, and there are more American banks with offices in London than New York. The question is, why. After World War II, America and Russia emerged the two contending hegemons. Of all qualifying powers or countries, which showed a hunger for international capital play, the City of London beat them all. While Paris suffered from Gaullist delusion and irascibility, on one hand, and a certain open anti-Americanism, Germany and Italy were too comatose and or suffered the odium of fascism to be admitted into the theatre. Of course, you have already guessed, then the world was Europe and Europe was the world.

Britain, which in itself at least, in 500 years, never had a history of pan-European bid for dominance, unlike virtually all others, played the card; she was only culturally related to America, but a considerably independent power. Of course, she had her UN Security Council seat to prove that. Even more, she easily thought of America as the new barbarian Rome, with her, Britain the sky soaring Attics (Greeks) of modern times. So, both Russia and China (the Red powers) felt safe keeping their cash with British bankers and the Americans, too. This play of vectors for which Britain, a nominally victorious power had no hands in, played in her favour. And the British, like our own Big Deltans, became a banking powerhouse, attracting a variety of financial services consumers, who just would not go anywhere else.

Space will not let us, we would have gone further to examine how Switzerland and even Austria also emerged as international banking havens, and further consolidate our thesis, that political weakness and or minority status are not entirely without their economic or banking advantages over dominant powers.

But before we conclude, let us invite Chinua Achebe and his Arrow of God. He writes of Umuaro, "They said that when the six villages first came together they offered the priesthood of Ulu to the weakest among them to ensure that none in the alliance became too powerful".

Within this gem of almost biblical purity is the heart of our thesis, that even in weakness there is certain sociology (market and power) strength, and we need not misdirect ourselves into thinking it is a conspiracy.

But what future this Deltan dominance? Perhaps, what happened to Ezeulu, Achebe's protagonist, would befall them if they do not understand and appropriately respond to the environment or sociological dynamics that drive their banking prowess, power and prosperity. Is business then all sociology and no strategy? No. But a misunderstanding or misapplication of the forces of nature or our sociology may mislead the bleeding strategist, however good or proficient.

And why is Delta State, the dominant banker, the Levite among the Israelites, in the greater Delta? It is also sociology of forces and we shall address that in subsequent essays.

It is not necessary or even expected that these bankers and their CEOs know of these forces. After all, they are only bankers, not practising sociologists or scholars. It is enough that they listen. Thus as the shifting waves of sociology and other non-market factors throw up new heroes and drown those afflicted with new dead weights, in her financial waters, there is nothing to mourn, but everything to understand.

POST SCRIPT: When we wrote: *But what future this Deltan dominance? Perhaps what happened to Ezeulu, Achebe's protagonist, would befall them if they don't understand and appropriately respond to the environment or sociological dynamics that drive their banking prowess, power and prosperity;* there is no need feeling gloated. But we foresaw the heavy regulatory and the reflexively punitive hammer that befell the Nigerian banking years before it happened. When Lamido Sanusi, then Central Bank Governor, sacked everybody, he was not doing banking. He was into geopolitical intervention. He wanted a geopolitical solution to the skewed, even if explainable, accumulation of banking assets by these greater Delta Turks.

If they had, however, listened to us, they would not perhaps have fallen victim to wildcat Sanusi. Even more, they would not have lived to a tragic denouement like Ezeulu as Achebe, who created him, did. It is not too late though. A new sociology of business audit and prognosis might save them greater errors as the future emerges.

However, one can observe that in spite of the political intervention the Big Delta or minority players are still a dominant financial power house. They control and run the new behemoth Zenith Bank; the fast rising Access Bank, and have substantial ownership and control grip on United Bank for Africa. These three banks alone are in the first four biggest banks bulge. And these four banks among themselves control about 70 per cent of Nigerian banking business.

One other issue that stuck out is the mixing up of ethnicity and geopolity and sociology as one by some readers. The example of Austria will serve us well. After World War II and the collapse of Germany, Austria was considered one of the international capitals of finance and diplomacy. This is something that was decidedly not granted Germany. OPEC, of course, has its headquarters at Vienna. And Austria was a bigger international centre for finance than Germany. All this is despite Austrians being ethnic Germans and that (the German) Hitler was actually an Austrian. Truth is that separate geography and boundaries gave the two cousins, different sociologies and more importantly different perceptions by competing world powers. Every belligerent power, even in peace, feared the Germans, yet the Austrian was wholly German.

So, it is important to understand that while some of the Big Deltans may be Igbo in part, their separate geopolitical mapping or classification and as those of the Austrians give them innocence not granted their Igbo heartland cousins. And this has market and financial implications.

4

Is There Then A Power Market, Too?

If my theory is correct then reality must conform to it.
The reality you know may be a dupe. Look well.
*Sharpen your eyes... - **Mother A'endu***

Yes, and the power market is also open to the sociology of power analysis. In the course of writing this essay some issues were raised by previewers and others who we sounded out. And it is important we attend to them. This is so that other readers who may be raising similar concerns will have them addressed before they so do. One of the reoccurring issues is that we were not sufficiently historical and that we skipped the contributions of important news media brands, and media big names like the Sketch, magazines like NewsWatch, Newbreed, New Nigerian, Daily Star, etc., and the Earnest Ikolis and Babatunde Joses of this world.

I suspect that this concern is from the traditional study of the media as its own existent, whole and entire. Media practitioners are often deluded they are objective almost android-like in the trade. And they make no other concessions. For many of them nothing other than objectivity and market savvy influence the making of great newspapers. In their implied logic the major papers The Sun, The Guardian, ThisDay, etc, are all doing well because of their professional vision and accomplishments. They cannot imagine any other outsider or outlier force at play. Perhaps, they are precociously right before the fact. After this perhaps, sociology of business analysis will be included as a standard market analysis, just as funds flow analysis currently is.

However, closer examination tells us media assets don't grow and flourish in its own world; that it is not one separate world, except in the sense in which it is one mesh of several worlds. We cannot just, like apartheid, live in our own Bantustans and separate existences. It is one grid, one motherboard.

The sociology of business analysis is an attempt to track a particular wire in a given motherboard. We therefore need not concern ourselves, distractively, with non-cognate details however weighty. Did Jose, for instance, achieve historical landmarks in the Nigerian media? And the answer is, yes. But that is extraneous to our purpose.

It is therefore important we repeat that we are not interested in a historical survey of the beginnings and growth of the media and media barons in Nigeria. And we implied so in the main essay by the cut-off point of the assumptions/illusions of being one, which was shattered by independence and civil war. Prior to self rule we all thought largely we were one. But for markets to exist we must have multiplicities of supplies and demands channels. A self sufficient economy, an autarky economy is not strictly a market or a market anybody is interested in here.

The splintering and or break up of Nigeria as a media, non monolithic market, came when self rule approached and we discovered we are not one people even if we are one nation. And then the dominant journalism was the journalism of anti-colonialism's wind of change. Let the British go home and grant us the leave to rule ourselves, we all cried.

Our interest is strictly and in this case to establish a fairly, perhaps, a wholly new business assessment tool and model that works in markets. And this is, that there is a sociology to the success of businesses in New York, Lagos or Nkwerre.

On the magazine sub-set, we skipped them because magazines for all their success are marginal media assets in Nigeria and by this, their owners and the magazines cannot count as dominant media moguls, or assets, which is our consideration. And to repeat, our claim is not that non-South-South nationals can't do well at all in the media asset owning business. Our claims are that the South-Southerners, by being minorities, have dividends and other compensatory assets attached to their numbers deficit. We have characterised this as the brace sector advantage. This is the first such classification in the world that we know of.

Incidentally, the magazines and their history support our positions. Perhaps, they just have to because there are no other options. To quote the respected media hand and watcher Mohammed Haruna: It (Newswatch magazine) did not start newsmagazine journalism in Nigeria. The credit for that must go to the since rested Newbreed, the gutsy biweekly the late, even more gutsy, Chief Chris Okolie (a minority) published from 1976. But even before Newbreed there was, of course, local magazine journalism. However, it was essentially entertainment and soft-sell oriented, led by publications like Drum, imported from South Africa, Spear and Woman's World published by Daily Times of Nigeria under the incomparable late Alhaji Babatunde Jose.

There was, in a sense, news magazine journalism of sorts even before Newbreed. Before Okolie, we had Africa (founded by Ralph Uwechue, another minority), Afriscope, West Africa, etc. But, except for Afriscope owned by Comrade, now Senator, Uche Chukwumerije, they were all published abroad, mostly from London. They were also monthly and, as their titles suggested, their scope of coverage was continental or sub-continental.

Newswatch may not have started news magazine journalism in Nigeria. However, the eternal credit for rediscovering that brand of journalism in the country even before Newbreed was to resume publication in 1987, seven years after the fatal ban military head of state, General Olusegun Obasanjo, imposed on it in 1978, must go to Newswatch. Not only did Newswatch rediscover news magazine journalism in Nigeria, it was the first to do so as a weekly. It was also the first print medium to be largely owned and controlled by journalists themselves.

The story of how the late Dele Giwa, Ray Ekpu, Yakubu Mohammed and Dan Agbese, dissatisfied with the integrity and credibility of journalism at their various publications, left to found a weekly news magazine of their own in late 1984 and subsequently publish it from February 28, 1985, has since become the stuff of legends.

By the time the four-some started their magazine they were all household names as journalists, editors and columnists. But as many an accomplished journalist, editor and columnist would attest to, their names were not enough to guarantee success. They also needed to work hard, publish and be damned and show clarity and simplicity in how they told and commented on their news stories. For years, week in, week out, they demonstrated all these qualities – and some – in the news and views they published.

Not surprisingly, within months their magazine caught the imagination of the Nigerian reading public and it became the reference point of Nigerian journalism, print and otherwise. (Daily Trust, September 19, 2012)

Actually, the men who founded Newswatch and Newbreed, the dominant magazine players in the times were/ are all minorities. And they, unlike their majority-persons, owned and or ran media assets, had command markets all over the country. This was in contrast to the majority-persons owned media brands like TheNews, considered by many as a South-West mouth propagandist motor mouth. It need not have been but the perception, which is all media assets are about, has market implications. Nobody, okay, not too many people believe TheNews, except in the South-West. And this reinforces the thesis that there is a minority dividend or if you like, blank cheque to their media asset promotion. The minorities have to be so reckless to overdraw a blank cheque.

And for media assets like Sketch, New Nigeria, Daily Star and Renaissance, we are not dealing at all with government intervention in the news marketplace. Governments by themselves are a monopoly/monopolistic and are uncompetitive. Thus it is not strange to assert that governments distort competition and do not enhance markets. The very idea of governments at play at the market is anti-market in the sense of a free market and is in part not in our consideration.

It is important though to understand that there is a market for politics, or that politics can be taken and examined, as a market, its own market. If we did, its demand and supply and price mechanisms are also determinable by the sociology of business or do we say sociology of politics models? Sociology of marketplaces is however and expectedly different from sociology of governments/electoral success, which we will at proper times fully address. Sociology of market success requires competitiveness and openness which is often not the case in government assets and play in the power game and marketplace. We do not want to mix the two here in any great detail but some hint will not be out of place.

Former Vice President Abubakar Atiku's confession, which made the headlines on September 19, 2012, in Mohammed's essay, is a pointer. According to the veteran politician, he opposed the six geopolitical zones canvassed for by former Vice President Alex Ekwueme on the fear that it was a hidden pro-Biafran breaking ploy. Not that it was or was not, but that was how he perceived it and that dictated his reaction and reception or otherwise of the idea. This tendency to be illogical at any time goes together with anyone is in power; that is, as a majority trait, it is human all too human. If Atiku and Ekwueme swapped positions, the same behaviour will also swap persons. It is not that Atiku is bad and evil and Ekwueme is good and excellent. It is just that their environments and assumptions as majority and minority persons. (The Igbo as a defeated people are political minorities and desperately want it all open, all fair and all inclusive). And Atiku and his people, the mindless victors (all victors are wont to be), want an exclusive arrangement, a very unitary Nigeria, at which whoever commands power at the centre becomes chief priest, emir, king, and philosopher. In fact, he becomes the people and the nation becomes him. And, of course, the North of which Atiku is a power prince by current arrangements, is the dominant, perhaps only power majority-peoples.

It is instructive that Atiku had to be a victim and loser in the power-shift game; that is, he becomes a minority, which is a man out of power, to be wise, to see to the truth that openness pays all, including Caesar. Instructively again, Atiku now as a minority political merchant wants the power game market all open all over again; he wants the six geopolitical zones, state police and banners, etc. Like Thucydides, Machiavelli and Trotsky, all outsiders to power as they wrote - minorities, defeated peoples, an Atiku - needed to lose in the power game to be wise. Perhaps, that is why for scholars to really know, to be great, have to be loners, outsiders to come to their own.

To repeat, the minorities being the weakest arm of/in the race to power can only find and found and augment strength in truth and openness. For them it is not a strategic opening; it is an existential necessity.

To possess or be burdened with the mindset of the victor is to lose out on cognitive assets. Famously, it is said there are no party intellectuals. To be in power is to be a blockhead, to be denied discernment. One cannot be an armed Caesar and a wise Buddha at the same time. And man must live by wisdom or he will quickly come to his evolutionary end and perish as specie. That is, the minorities are essential for our continued existence as man or nation or community.

This explains in part why New Nigerian quickly came to their best buy date and could sociologically no longer survive. Only a new New Nigerian can. The old is dead with the sociology that once propped her up. And this explains, to quote Mohammed; The story of how the late Dele Giwa, Ray Ekpu, Yakubu Mohammed and Dan Agbese, dissatisfied with the integrity and credibility of journalism at their various publications, left to found a weekly news magazine of their own in late 1984.

This dissatisfaction of the minority on and about the integrity and credibility is against the attempt by majority peoples to rig any medium available to them to deliver a given message. That message is that their will to rule is a mandate of heaven. And this will to rule excludes the minority persons, except as patronising presences. No minority talent can make it to the top in such enclosures. Theirs is to be courtiers, millionaire shoe-shiners, court eunuchs, but not kings or even princes.

To consolidate and take the thesis across the business frontier to the political marketplace: Minorities are not just of numbers but generically those out of the power loop because of, or despite their numbers. A majority peoples are those in power and need not necessarily be in the greater numbers. It is just that greater numbers, in power assets or whatever else, count, predisposes to greater power, to the delusion of possessing a blank cheque, politically or otherwise. Arab dictatorships are model examples of this conundrum.

5

South-South: Braced
For Competitive Dominance?

Now, we hope we have made it clear that the media, the banking and the humour and related businesses here named: Brace or Connective business sectors are like most businesses sociology of business advantage or a sociological turf endowment. It follows that the whole concept of sociology of business should be understood and practically delineated to serve and service the South-South, as a minority geo-polity, and others the most it can. And more particularly the concept of brace and non-brace economic sectors should be understood and embraced by our South-South economic thinkers to jump start development with much traction. The slogan perhaps should read: South-South, Braced up for Competitive Advantage or Dominance!

To make brace and non-brace business sectors clear, let us inquire into the business of classifications. Generally, businesses are classified by some logic or another. It could be by the nature of the products, their manufacturing or their markets. We have consumer goods, industrial equipment goods; service and manufacturing sectors, etc. We also have for marketers, fast moving consumer goods, premium brands, etc. We also have for econometricians, goods with elastic demands and goods with inelastic demands.

All are valid and each in its case emphasises one or some particular product cleavages and asset curves. It is similar to a fashionable lady's wardrobe, which emphasises clothes that market and enhance her curves and bumps the best. A trendy size-plus lady need not acquire an Agbani Darego-style wardrobe. Mere classification and or reclassification could help a hitherto weak competitor, in fashion, industry, or indeed in just any competitive or conflict scenario, emerge competitively viable big cat, and on its own terms.

Usually if a particular product line so grows that it constitutes 30 per cent plus of the total volume or value of its sector, it has constituted a new business sector. Notable examples are oil and gas, which in most bourses, is categorised as unique. Oil and gas are properly speaking commodities. And computers started life as office equipment. They have grown so unwieldy they have to stand on their own. And all these reclassifications are, as it were, self-fulfilling or empowering prophecies. The most famous in history may be those of the Jews whose priests cleverly reclassified their people as the elect of God and the others as Gentiles, the non-elect of God.

That is, there is nothing sacrosanct about the classifications. They all suffer shifting borders and aggregations. Classifications are there to serve man, the economic animal and not the economic man, classifications. That is, we should never be shy to invent, extend and innovate categories and classifications. There is only one provision. And it is that it be rational and serves useful economic and possibly other purposes. All classifications are valid that are in themselves rational and self-consistent in their logic.

If we classified economy into two broad categories of brace and non-brace or more properly, constitutive and connective sectors, we would serve our South-South, and indeed all minority-peoples, a great new economic vision. This vision is convertible to decisive market advantage and assets. Additionally, the innovation will help explain, as traditional classifications and economics cannot, our legendary self-ignorance. This particular feature, of coming to acute self knowledge, will all too plausibly ward off a certain imminent civil war. Hints, if not declaration of impending war, has been going on quietly and we are as usual not able to read the early signs of this death-bearing call.

THE RISKS

Ignorance is itself a state of cognitive disorder and asymmetry. Ignorance in a world of conflict or competition is quick to result in a state of war. And as it is indicated it is nearly as disruptive, destructive of a people and their community, as her shooting variant. And we are as warlike as we are ignorant.

And just as the day will come when a single carrot, freshly observed, will set off a revolution, surely the day will also come, when an ancient conundrum freshly understood, can stop a war. Stopping an about-to-happen civil war or just any other tragedy by untying and understanding an ancient conundrum is a key aim of our game, of the scholar☐s game.

THE LAW

Generally, it can be said that where parties of variant sizes are in competition; that is, majority asset or endowment and minority asset or endowment parties, are in completion the minority parties, that is the South-Southerners in the Nigerian example, will dominate any business that braces the people together, or will dominate the common spaces. Why? And the answer is that the sociology of business advantage is in their favour. And the sociology of business is the terrain of competition. That is, the South-South owns the ground advantage in this specific instance of brace businesses. And we can, as Ernest Hemmingway said, it is a moveable ground advantage. That is, wherever the South-Southerner goes, the ground advantage goes with him. And the advantage holds whether the competition is for power or for profit or whatever else. In whatever braces the parties together, that is the advantaged ground of the minority parties.

What to Do

The most urgent task is for us to fully understand and tap into the existential and or structural advantages of the South-South to accelerate her development and perhaps act as an engine to the economic wagon that is the country. That is, what the South-South is now as never called to do.

And our thinking is further suggested by the position of one of China's great economists, Professor Justin Yifu Lin. We quote from his paper: Development 3.0 Today, a 'Development Economics 3.0' is needed.

In my view, the shift from understanding the determinants of a country's economic structure and facilitating its change is tantamount to throwing the baby out with the bath water. Remember that Adam Smith called his great work An Inquiry into the Nature and Causes of the Wealth of Nations. In a similar spirit, development economics should be built on inquiries into the nature and causes of modern economic growth - that is, on structural change in the process of economic development.

In my book New Structural Economics, I propose shifting the focus to areas where developing countries can do well (their comparative advantages) based on what they have (their endowments). With dynamic structural change starting from there, success will breed success.

If a country's firms can do that, the economy will be competitive, capital will accumulate quickly, the endowment structure will change, areas of comparative advantages will shift, and the economy will need to upgrade its industrial structure to a relatively higher level of capital intensity. So successful industrial upgrading and economic diversification requires first-movers, and improvements in skills, logistics, transportation, access to finance, and various other changes, many of which are beyond the first-movers□ capacity. Governments need to provide adequate incentives to encourage first-movers, and should play an active role in providing the required improvements or coordinating private firms' investments in those areas.

The best the South-South or minority parties, in variant sizes, party completions can do is to identify those brace-businesses, where they have home-run advantages and functionally and formally dominate them. Then from there they can move into greener or constitutive sectors and other pastures. This will leave the minority parties, a South-South as an example, an unbeatable force for economic, business and other good. In a word, it will make of them competitive overlords if not dominating the majority parties, at least, acquire more competitive weight than their size should rationally or proportionally indicate.

Even more the South-South should come to knowledge that the minorities are a nation's most vibrant creative belt. Per capita, the South-South minorities have beaten us all in creative enterprises. From sports to newspapering, to humour they are on top of the game. It is as it should be. Generally, the most creative people are the minority peoples, the outsiders. This is whether they are of the majority tribes or not. To create, to be most creative, it is generally recognised you need to be a minority, the outsider. Thus, a Soyinka, an Achebe, and a Dan Maraya Jos are not strictly speaking Yoruba or Igbo or Hausa. He is an outsider to his society. That is why each has those deep and resonant views.

In a sense, therefore, Achebe and Soyinka are minority party geniuses. In fact, they have to be to be geniuses at all. That is genius, which is a synonym for high-sensitivity achievement, may also be classified as structurally a minority party asset. It is an insight that can with appropriate tools be commercialised with huge benefits reaped.

But the minority of the South-South is structural, founded by history, like those of the Jews, before modern Israel was founded. What is needed is to formalise this structure into an economic, scientific and existential advantage and gift as the Jews did.

6

As The Drum Beat And Summon The Tribes To A New Bloodbath

How do you justify the fact that most of the banks are owned by the people from the South-South? How do you justify the situation where most of the media houses are owned by people from the South-South? You think that they are the hardest workers?

-Arewa Consultative Forum, ACF

Meanwhile, we must not allow the irredentists - Northerners, South-Westerners, South-Easterners or whoever - to beat war-drums against the South-South people by false and unfounded claims. And one of the most virulent examples of this false claim is that the South-South dominates the media and banking because of free oil money, which is old and subsisting peddling of ignorance. All we have tried to do is to retire this wondrous unknowing and bring in new understanding.

Wars are driven by gratuitous or purposed ignorance. That is why hotlines were established to clear the fog between wise men who are in the dangerous game of power. All we are doing is to debunk this sweet and all-too believable lie against the South-South, an innocent minority peoples. And to alert us that coups are mini wars, wars in full character, but in mini forms. Coups are mini wars waged against a country by a successful military faction.

But before the coup as in wars, the sympathetic media will be full of alarms of weapons of mass destruction or unearned sectional control of the mass media, banking, and industrial assets. Such claims can lead to coup and a sectional army will invade the political scene allegedly to redeem the nation or what remains of her. But its real and true mission is a sectional agenda, to ambush and seize by guns and for its sections what others earned by votes, enterprise, etc.

The entry strategy of the new coup makers will come in the form of nationalising the South-South media. Or perhaps to demand that the South-South founder's equity be diluted, shared out and donated to others who never worked for it. The example of bank directorships and assets which were forcefully divested and shared out on federal character basis, among others, are still in recent historical memory. And one may easily recall the words of Ayo Opadokun, a prominent leader of the Yoruba: From October 1985, Yoruba leaders and captains of industries and professionals, particularly many in the Metropolitan Club, had persistently sent emissaries to Chief Awolowo, pleading with him to intervene over the raw deal they were suffering in their various business activities. Such emissaries were initially facilitated by Prince Babs Oyekanmi. For example, they lamented that they were having difficulty securing government approval for some of their business requirements, except when they enlisted one or two far Northerners into their board membership. They sought a meeting with Papa in the greatest interest of the Yoruba nation. (Posted on Sahara Reporters, August 13, 2012), as 'Awo And His Politics: A Silver Jubilee Intimate Reminiscence' By Ayo Opadokun. It is now time to ronu.

Before we war-war, let us sue for a little more knowledge, especially a little new knowledge. A people are as ignorant as they are warlike and vice versa. Cure ignorance and you would have banished rancour, coups, if not all-out shooting wars. Only knowledge makes us less beastly. Only new knowledge may explain ancient mysteries, disabuse long held prejudices and grudges and leave us safer than we found the world.

PART TWO:

Part Two:

7

ABC Of Transport: It's Sociology Of Business Stupid!

If we are to believe Nassim Nicholas Taleb, motivational speaker and author of self-help, or How to be a Millionaire books are all trading in charlatanism. Anyway, the great Wall Street financial mathematician looked at the best of such authors and passed the verdict. In some sense he may be right, especially if we sat back and checked thoroughly on the plausibility of the "good news" of these do-good authors.

But fair is fair; we have to grant the best of them some genius. And this genius lies in one simple fact. They recognised, perhaps more than anybody else, that in the market place, a good suit is priced higher than a good brain... and that buzz words command more fees than the truth on Broad Street.

So they armed themselves with those and a certain astonishing capacity at presentation skills. On and given a podium, these men can be as electrifying as sparks of diamonds, and fool any audience into ardent believer-ship.

Perhaps, in an economy as down as Nigeria's we need many of them, if only to keep the un-employment queue shortened. For in the end, these men, with How to be millionaire elixirs, end up making only themselves the millionaires.

On a certain Saturday evening, my friend Professor J. A. E. Obuekunnie visited from New York. For lack of something better to do, I took him to one of these How to and inspirational live talk shows. And the master, after we paid admission fees, spoke about the skills of the owners of ABC Transport and Ekene Dili Chukwu among others.

After the "show" Professor Obuekunnie confronted him personally and asked a few questions. Firstly, was the opportunity to be Chief Augustine Ilodibe, founder of the Ekene Dili Chukwu Transport, open to all regardless of place of domicile and host society?

But the How to be a millionaire master insisted that strategy transcended sociology. But does it? This was the question Obuekunnie asked but I had no answer, so he had to provide one. I think is it is a thesis worth listening to or reading. I transcribe:

"You see, despite this feel-good, yes-we-can thesis, business is as much circumscribed as it is affected by a people□s sociology. The question he misses to ask is, why must Ekene come from Nnewi, ABC from Mbaise and Young from Neni? The truth is that he does not even know it is a subject area. For him it is all strategy, but strategy does not act in a vacuum. It needs a reality, and that reality is as important, if not more so than anything else. It is also fair to acknowledge that business or the pursuit of profit will of itself interface, circumscribe and shape the sociology of a people.

"Wal-Mart is a famous example in America, so also in the computer as a business tool, and transportation in Nigeria and the rest of the world. You see, our friend would not know that the chances of an Ekene not coming from Nnewi was as near zero as it was possible within the greater Igbo universe. Now, this is a snap history of business in Igbo land. Besides Abiriba, in Abia State, Nnewi is one of the most, possibly the most successful entrepreneurial Igbo town and peoples.

"While Abiriba was like an oasis, with Igbere and Item, as weak tributary satellites, Nnewi was like the epicentre of an entrepreneurial outflow, covering Utuh, Amichi, Ozobulu. While the Nnewi commercial conurbation generated a certain mass and momentum, its Abiriba equivalent was self-isolating or even reclusive. Why we may ask? Our immediate instincts point to a stand-alone or largely unique Abiriba-area matrilinealism within the Igbo universe. And because of the ensuing inheritance mismatch, this did not quite allow for any meaningful spousal or commercial intercourse between the Abiriba Igbos and their patriarchal neighbours, as was the case with Nnewi.

"What happened was that as the Nnewi merchants "moved" into new territories, Onitsha emerged as a "take off" capital and export port. This move saw the greater Nnewi merchants spread as far north as Kano and Maiduguri, as far West as Lagos and Ibadan and in the East, Aba, and Port Harcourt were also home and hunting grounds.

"Without intending it, a certain need for transportation, for men, material and goods developed. At first it was subsidiary need and industry, servicing directly the trading community. Of course, this need will be first picked up by insiders, who, in wanting to move their goods, may decide to buy lorries or rent some.

"And in those days the Nnewi merchant was head and shoulders above his competitors, and had accumulated some un-matched capital. Thus it was natural for him to sense that the transportation needs of his and others could be turned into a business of its own.

"Next came the battle of wits, gifts and strategy. And this was practically if not ideally suited for those within the charmed circle... the traders themselves, who first lived the need. Not just that the typical Nnewi trader was bigger and more successful than his competitors, he had other members of his greater Nnewi constituency as first or even captive market. This gives him, an Ekene Dili Chukwu say, a critical edge that cannot be available to another from or resident at Nsukka, say".

But no kingdom lasts forever. With the coming of the civil war, the greater Nnewi business community suffered like the rest of Igbo land. After the war, they made, outside the Abiribas, the quickest recovery.

While the Abiriba recovery can be accounted for by their repatriation of cash and capital from the West Coast where they were and have been a significant economic force, the Nnewi recovery, despite the robbery of all Igbo by the Federal Government by the obnoxious (£20.00) twenty pounds policy led by the dictator General Jack Gowon and championed by Chief Obafemi Awolowo, was aided by their property holdings and track records, with local banks and suppliers abroad.

Meanwhile, other Igbo after the war, with a sense of liberation, plunged into business, learning and competing with the Nnewis. By the 1980s, it was clear that Nnewi leadership in (Igbo) business was only in quantitative and was no longer sustainable in qualitative terms. All the "tricks" of doing business and making a killing in the marketplace seem to have been passed around, especially in all Anambra.

Before now, the biggest motor spare parts seller was likely or even had to be from Nnewi; so also the biggest yam seller, and just about anything in between. The Abiribas were the biggest, but only in their specialised or captive areas of stockfish, okrika and linen.

Thus the very nature of the game had changed, especially in its sociology and demographics. Before this change, for instance, and expectedly the biggest long distance luxury operators were all from Nnewi; viz Ekene Dili Chukwu, Izu Chukwu and Chidi Ebere Transport Services.

But as we write the reality has thrown up a Young Shall Grow Motors as the indisputable number one, with just about anybody who can, to be number two, wherever he comes from, especially within a critical Anambra entrepreneurial zone. More on this later.

So in the sociology of business terms what happened? What happened is that as the spread and reach of business and money making touched all Igbo land, and Anambra especially, the relative weight and densities of the Nnewi phenomenon logically diminished. And with a diminished presence, the market was now open to all Igbo but especially the Anambra

Igbo who now lead, as Nnewi once led all Igbo.

It was only with the realignment of sociological forces, if you won't mind, that the genius of a Young Shall Grow had to find expression. If his "people", the non-Nnewi Anambra, were not in the "trade of things", chances are he would have missed that "instinctive", non-Blackberry calculatable feel, to make him access (1) market and need intelligences, (2) their very changing nature and texture etc, and take a plunge, or even profit by responding adequately as changing market circumstances and intelligence dictate.

And now what about ABC Transport? ABC Transport is the case of a niche that is as sociological, if not more so... In fact, it is than it is business strategy.

Again as we write, Mbaise is the single largest pool of technocratic, civil service and corporate players in Igbo land. Of course, part of this is explainable by their penchant for education. But even more than this is in their "safety of numbers". Mbaise remains one of the most populous Igbo sub-clans.

When you add to the Mbaises their neighbours and cousins, the Owerris, who are no less educated, then you have the largest pool of that given demographic class. That is, Igbo, who are not traders, but workers, spread and scattered all over the federation.

Now the founder of ABC Transport is an Mbaise man, so the link begins to emerge. What would have happened is that, as an educated people, he and his friends, brothers, towns and community people would have "felt bad" on the luxury bus service provided by Anambra entrepreneurs essentially, even if not so stated, to serve the interest of the traders.

At the back of the mind of ABC's founder, Mr. Frank Nneji, will be a lot of sighs... 'how bad I am treated'. Added to this will also be the sighs and cacophony of his other Mbaise and Owerri clan educated commuters. It is only after this that his mind would have done that "blackberry free" calculation, that here is a chance to seize the day.

So, when he founded ABC it was to service his kind of travel needs which is prevalent in commercial quantities among his clans. Today ABC serves this style of educated non-trading community wherever they come from. But the point is to understand that whatever strategy he had sprouted from a certain sociology and abundance of local condition. If you are excluded or you exclude yourself from this local condition, the chance that strategy will save you is nearer zero than infinity.

It is sociology stupid. Go to the ants and learn. And lastly, one final word. It does not mean that either the ABC Motors or Young Shall Grow founders or their Ekene counterparts are consciously aware of these (sublimely and subconscious) facts and verities. They, of course, are businessmen, not scholars or sociologists, and we may not expect them to know. In fact, it may simply be beyond them. "Doing business and knowing business" are separate things, and the twain may not meet in one man.

8

Brand Deconstruction:
Is Branding The Last Portal Of
Imperialism?

*We are all safer and indeed healthier
dead than alive, living a lie.*

-Queen Mother A'endu

Is Biodun Shobanjo, Chairman Troyka Communications Group, Lagos, an agent of imperialism? What of Dr. Chuka Nwosu, Chairman, Black and Proud Group, Enugu, practitioners of the communications trade. Is he not a factor for neo-imperialism? Truth is, they and their tribe of industry players may all be, even without intending or knowing it.

Now, if one visited Adland or the world of marketing communications as the current usage dictates the hottest buzz word is about branding. It is branding stupid, every practitioner solemnly proclaims. It is so all pervasive that today all it takes to be a hot button product or personnel is to be characterized in brand-speak. Fancy words like brand equity, brand DNA, brand and product convergence are used to seduce the laity and sound very self important besides the demand for exaggerated fees.

However, if one cared to read the minutes of the last meeting he will readily notice the following. It is that like the latest 7 Series BMW, iPod or the Windows 7, Hyundai car, branding as a concept and service value is an imported product category. And it is imported from North America and Europe, unlike Hyundai say, which is from Asia. Matters look harmless but they are not. If one read the minutes further one will notice that despite a certain diffidence to talk, truth is that branding is a very recent phenomenon or discovery. Branding was not always there with us. In fact, according to Wikipedia: My argument is that modern branding as a discipline is only 50+ years old, and that almost all the theories and methodologies regarding branding are derived from that period. This means that nothing is set in stone, and in fact it's quite likely that branding as a discipline is still in the "flat earth" stage.

That puts modern branding as a phenomenon of the 1960s. A further and careful examination and reading of the last minutes tells us that that is not a very innocent date. Now this; before World War I it was trite knowledge that the European was leading, and in nearly all departments, the human race. However, a jolt was given to this by the Russo-Japanese war in which the Japanese Yellow Peril subdued the White supremacist certainty for the Russians and other Westerners. Before this there were the victories of Genghis Khan, but those were taken as flukes and at best ancient history; that is, well before this present, new, Darwinian and best evolved European/Whiteman. Of course, World War II saw Japan achieve spectacular victories, especially against the British. However, the Japanese bid for an Asia-wide empire collapsed in her final defeat. The defeat of the Japanese almost in spite of itself suggested the ultimate superiority of the white race.

But something else happened. In a miracle of non-Western and but wholly human achievement, the Japanese came back from the horrors and humiliation of defeat and raced ahead to overtake virtually all Western countries in 1000 and one areas of manufacturing. From steel to cameras, from cars to white goods the Japanese beat them all. Using the Toyota marquee as an example, the Japanese trumped the Detroit car makers in almost all indices including price, reliability and fuel consumption. The Japanese also beat the mythical Germans at the camera and other optical equipment businesses. Venerable German names like Leica, Zeiss camera and other optical brands could not compete with the Canons at the market place and quickly disappeared or almost. Quick to follow were the Italian motorcycle or scooter business, trounced by Honda and other then Japanese upstarts.

This unexpected Japanese victory brought with her a period of soul searching and shaken confidence in Europe and the West. Part of European/Western response was to send scholars to study the Japanese and articulate a pattern of defence. Following was a surge of books explaining Japan and her management style, of which Theory Z by William G. Ouchi became something of a classic, transcending the initial impulse. Also, Japanese books or inspired books became worldwide bestsellers. Sun Tzu's The Art of War (a Chinese war manual, re-couched as a business primer by the Japanese genius for adaptation and reinterpretation) became a global bestseller. All these soul searching started in the late 1960s at the first high of Japanese trouncing of the West at their own boardroom games.

That is, there is a coincidence of dates... the West wanted a change when the Japanese beat them at it. That is, prior to the 1960s when manufacturing excellence was a European/ Western forte and monopoly, the world was so promoted and ordered that the Holy Grail was engineering excellence. Of course, the West never expected or planned there will be any change in this Western-led engineering excellence and fixed order of things; the West, it was expected, will remain the engineering and manufacturing top cats. But change came and unexpectedly and the West was rattled.

To take on the Japanese challenge, after several false and failed attempts, the West continued the war by other means, and justifiably, one would say. Branding was one of it. (Others could be the Western charge of unfair trading practices by the Japanese, negotiated export quotas, manipulation of dollar/ Western currency exchange rates, etc, which may be classed as the diplomatic front of the war. But these need not concern us here).

But the West, by this strategic detour, out-flanked the Japanese from where they least expected it, as it were, an intellectual Leyte. Deploying the intellectual armoury where they still have a decisive edge, the West shifted the battle off the boardrooms to the faculty halls. Here Harvard, Yale and Oxford reign supreme and unchallenged. In fact, we are told the top 20 universities in the world are essentially the preserve of the United States and the United Kingdom, two cousin nations, if there was one. Of the remaining 80 in the top 100 the West's dominance is still overwhelming.

Theoretically, if there is any place where objective disinterestedness is observed it is in the academia. And Harvard, Sorbonne and Oxford are the epitome of all it is to be objective, the best and brightest in academics. But are they? Perhaps, it will be after Christ or the end of history has come. For now the reality is that we are all partisans even without intending or knowing it. The fact of the partisanship is well documented even if conveniently and all too humanly overlooked. Perhaps, the historian E. H. Carr has some handle on it. He writes, Germany's dramatic rise to power in the sixties and seventies of last century was impressive enough to make the leading British philosophers of the next generation-Card, T. H. Green... ardent Hegelians. Thereafter, the Kaiser's telegram to Kruger and the German naval programme spread the conviction among British thinkers that Hegel was a less good philosopher than had been supposed; and since 1914 no British philosopher of repute has ventured to sail under the Hegelian flag...

Nor is it only professional thinkers who are subject to such influences. Popular opinion is not less markedly dominated by them... some years later, "the gallant little Japs" of 1905 underwent a converse metamorphosis into "the Prussian of the East."... it is symptomatic that most people, when challenged, will indignantly deny that they form their opinions in this way; for as Acton long ago observed, "few discoveries are more irritating than those which expose the pedigree of ideas." (The Twenty Years' Crisis 1919-1939)

However, we will give it to Walter Kaufmann to pinpoint the ways and recruitment of these apparently objective men into partisanship and as foot soldiers or commanding Generals; there are many reasons for Nietzsche's being one of the great scapegoats of all time, he writes in his introduction to On the Genealogy of Morals. Continuing, During World War I, British intellectuals found it convenient to contribute to the war effort by denouncing a German intellectual of stature whom one could discuss in print without losing a lot of time reading him-and Nietzsche had said many nasty things about the British. Henceforth Nietzsche was a marked man, and World War II contributed its share to this type of disgraceful literature. It is common knowledge, for instance, that all through the World War II that Western and especially British and American newspapers and statesmen and generals spoke glowingly or disparagingly of Stalin depending on the state or perception of Russia's strategic usefulness to Western war aims as the contribution to victory.

The critical point and phrase to note is contribution to the war effort and or victory. It is thus obvious intellectuals, artists and, worst of all, newspapermen, are not innocent bystanders or objective observers to the events and wars of their times. They can be hired, conscripted or even voluntarily enlist even without apparently knowing it. Things happen. And as the Japan has educated the rest of us, the boardroom is also a theatre of war and not just for commercial deliberations. And that one can make up for his loss in the war theatre with gains in the boardrooms and market places. Perhaps, this gave the Western scholars the good conscience they needed to join the fray on behalf of their tribal industrial groupings against the Japanese and the rest of the world. In a sense, and like we earlier remarked, this intellection-driven Leyte-like manoeuvre helped rout the Japanese all over again, even if not completely, as General MacArthur once did.

The fact that is implied in all these is that if the Japanese had not shredded the myth of White superiority in industry and manufacturing, the West and her scholars would not have invented or had need to invent branding as a tool of competitive warfare. Perhaps, just as Einstein confessed he would not have gone ahead with the atomic bomb if he had known the Nazis were not after all up to it; need and survival drive even our greatest intellectual engagements. Now while an Einstein is a self conscious actor, a great majority of others, in no way geniuses by the way, are not necessarily so.

Before now it was Western and especially German engineering excellence and technical superiority that allowed the West to dominate the world's markets for produced goods. Thus it was something of moral apostasy for the same West to now assert and brand Seiko watches as the poor man's Rolex, and quite unnecessarily if you consider the basis of Western/German penetration and domination of the global markets have hitherto been couched in terms of their engineering Excellencies. Branding Zaitech and not engineering excellence routed Seiko (technically as cutting edge as Rolex) as a poor and less margin earning product, thus making the West earn more kobo for her excellence than her Japanese counterparts, for an engineered product of similar exquisiteness, qualities and capacities.

***

History does not have a Petri-dish, but if the Western dominance in engineering had not been broken and shattered by the Japanese, a Seiko produced by, say an emerging Ireland, would have within a Western design assumption, sold worldwide as delivering more value and time for its price than the over-priced Rolex... that if it were an intra-Western commercial world war. And Rolex would have rather been branded an over-priced Seiko. Gradually, an Ireland-made Seiko would, like Mercedes, earn premium dollar and displace all others, including the Rolex in the Western shaped universe and zeitgeist.

(If we extend the insights of Thomas S. Kuhn [The Structure of Scientific Revolutions] a little, then there is nothing sacred or fixed about paradigm shifts; their courses are not prefixed. It is a triumphant convention among other competing conventions. Truth is perhaps the/our most convenient lies. Or the least harmful lies of the most powerful. Or the least harmful lies of the most powerful that works in its while till its sustenance power falls. Perhaps, a new daylight will shine into the darkness of old magic when Harvard is replaced by University of Hong Kong and Yale by Seoul National University as the new paradigm/ideas factories of the world. The idea that branding is the logical and inevitable development of the world of marketing or consumer value is at best a lie. That the logic of service or engineering excellence would have served the world and its market just as well and perhaps even better must be contemplated if not believed).

And the more the non Japanese-Asians joined to trounce the West the greater the fury and eruption in branding as an intellectual war tool for the Harvard-led alliance against the Axis powers of coming up peoples. In the face of their rampaging market and manufacturing excellence, a Japan was later, if reluctantly thought and admitted as an arm of the Western-driven alliance against the rest of the world. Even the Japanese themselves believed it (Triad Power by Kenichi Ohmae) and Japan was consequently characterised and thought of as a quirk and a stand-alone. To confirm the myth of the so-called unique Japanese soul, even among Asians, this exceptionalism was being rigorously canvassed and believed. And Japan was designated non-replicable and unique oddity. Apartheid South Africa even waded in and excused the Japanese as Honorary White men.

The alarm, however, blew when the so-called unique Japanese soul and manufacturing excellence, which was at par with those of Europe and North America devolved and rippled down the whole of the Confucian/Hindustan basin. In response branding became a new and high intensity necessity for the Western warrior scholars and their sponsoring entrepreneurs. And as a follow-up they exported it to the world, especially their captive colonial markets of joyfully ignorant and never thinking Africa.

We are not saying branding is not a legitimate war tool. After all, all is fair in war as in love as our own Chief Obafemi Awolowo stood on that, to starve, as a co-conspirator with General Yakubu Gowon, millions of Igbo civilians, children, women, pregnant women to death and with good conscience. The important thing is to come to knowledge and know how it all began. It is not that our practitioners should rebel and abandon their fat and fattening fees, sense of self-importance or even commercial epiphany. No, it is just that they need to understand how it all began or as the Chinese would say, when you drink water think of its source. And perhaps through this understanding we will all come to knowledge, as Mother A'endu would say, that things don't just sprout, they first take roots.

Thus the development of advertising or marketing communications practice and theory needed not to have, in necessity, led to branding as a paradigm path. Other paths could have been appropriately invented or the old ones retained and perhaps sharpened. That is, that the West's chosen branding paradigm path is contingent on a number of factors, the most basic of which is the containment of the manufacturing excellence of Asia. And this is especially as she enlarges and envelopes more and more countries.

The outcome of this highly successful intellectual war manoeuvre is quite telling; now because of the dismissal of engineering excellence, upon which the West built its dominance and the dramatic turn to branding you will notice the following; if you goggled 100 Greatest Brands they are all essentially Western and the top 10 are all American. (Of course, there is no 100 top engineered commodities list known to this author). It is not all a harmless coincidence; it is essentially the booty and spoils of colonial and neo-imperialistic war won not by Maxim guns but by Harvard wonks. The possession of the intellection Maxim guns is so strategically overwhelming that the West is the inventor and clearing house for categories. Concepts and categories like BRICs (Jim O'Neil of Goldman Sachs) and emerging markets (Antoine van Agtmael) are actually the invention of Western bankers and academics and exported to the agenda countries or regions. The West also is the world's cultural clearing house. In Nigeria and one believes, much of the Third World too, (another Western category) Sun Tzu's The Art of War, is read as a Western text actually or at worst a Western approved primer, with its Sino-Japanese origins assumed almost non-existent.

What the West did and deployed is the tactics of the crocodile. Immediately she battles and grabs her prey on the land, her next move is to drag her antagonist to the waters where she, the croc has supreme advantage and competence; and would just begin by drowning the contender-antagonist almost effortlessly. And as the Igbo say, out there in the waters the croc merits her name as the lion (supreme hunter) of the sea... agu-iyi. Intellectually, the West is the croc in its waters, the agu-iyi of the world; top hunter and predator and top of the cultural food chain. It will easily beat any antagonist-contender humiliatingly here. And this strategic war imbalance will remain to the West's favour until, perhaps, a new daylight enters into the old magic and Harvard is replaced by University of Hong Kong and Yale by Seoul National University as the new paradigm/new ideas factories of the world; and this, coupling the manufacturing excellence for which the Asians have beaten the Whites.

Now, if we used the price-engineering-excellence ratios and drew up the top 100, the West may trounce the Asians but not anywhere as badly and as totally as with and in the top 100 brands. Just by dragging the war to a new turf, that is, intellectual waters, the West, like the ancient and wise agu-iyi, crushes the rest of us even without our knowing it, in fact with our thanking them for the discovery of our easy path to uncompetitive ruin, if not death.

If the contest was intra-West the rules of engagement would have been different. But in being trans-West other and newer rules are added. It is not entirely a Western man's perversity if perversity it is. Just as a Chief Obafemi Awolowo* (and his co-accomplice General Yakubu Gowon) would not have deployed the tools of genocide and mass starvation of the innocent if it was an intra-Yoruba or intra-Hausa-Fulani/North civil war. But luckily the starved-to-death is not their dead and might as well be as good as a heap of butchered cattle for McDonalds or Mr Biggs. (According Awolowo the epithet of a sage, or Gowon of a man of peace, is nothing but an elegant form of genocide denial, of re-branding to win a new war. History is a record of what happened and not what we wished happened or a victor's sole narrative).

***

If the come comes to become, history, we repeat, comes with no Petri-dish and we can only imagine things out. But whenever it is the turfs change, it seems we also change the rules if not the entire game, if only to ensure we win the trophy. Perhaps, it is only when and if happily the world truly becomes one will there be less and less human harm and chicanery. Of the era it may be supposed that true history will be recorded and there will not be need to jump across logic as it suits us, temporarily. And this is whether it is in the politics, business or branding matters.

All what the branding war has done is to extend the shelf life of imperialism even if only by minutes. And the West has been successful at that as some of our best and brightest brains fall over themselves to brand. Professor Dora Akunyili as Information Minister once spent billions even when she or just about anybody else about her, had no idea what/where branding really is or began. But it is all right; at least, there are the fat fees to console these portal keepers of Western neo-imperialism or those of local victors, disguised as Broad Street tycoons or patriotic mandarins, citizens and politicians.

Tragically, Africa is not in the war like the two great contending powers of Asia and Europe/North America, but they are not unaffected bystanders. Whoever wins will imperialise Africa all over again for being such intellectual pigmies and engineering non-starters, despite our bloated but diseased self importance. And all this is traceable to a certain branded ignorance of even our greatest men, who go out of their way to canvass that the problem with Nigeria is simply and squarely a problem of leadership. Careful investigation reveals that the assertion has its provenance in Europe (see our essay; Why only the Americans could have invented the computer). Leadership, however, is the least of our problems. Our biggest problem is rather our monumental inability to think; our readiness to import our most fancied goods finished, including finished thoughts and thought forms from the West, including branding, without further inquiry or investigation. Perhaps, ignorance is bliss, especially commercial bliss, or so we think when we are poorer for it.

Cultural hegemony, of which the exportation of metropolitan or the victor-driven categories, is, perhaps, her finest expression (ideas, religions and intellectual fads) are able to net in provincial national recruits as evangelisers in complete innocence for both parties. It is achieved in such a bewitching manner that these volunteering-recruits do not suspect in the least that they are vectors of metropolitan and other peoples' partisanships. It is not just the pay, though that is important, especially as the metropolis pays best, sometimes with offices or admittance into Western privileges. In fact, these local recruits of foreign commercial powers often pride themselves as objective, universal men and all too palpably part of the new elect, bearers, keepers and hawkers of the new magical flame.

Ironically, it also so happens that sometimes the victim, political, commercial or otherwise, persuades and convinces himself he is a free agent and even an elect of history and chance. For an illustration, Professor Achebe, apparently in a near complete shutdown of nerves, beatifies an un-confessed murderer and genocidist, Malam Aminu Kano, as a saint, a saintly man? [Next December 12, 2010]. Is it not more than error enough, one wonders that earlier, he, Achebe, chose to hunt for power and pick votes with the same Aminu Kano? (Or did he confess and apologise privately to Achebe? Things happen!). Maybe our earlier and even criminal silences egged and pushed him on. It was indeed criminal of us to have kept silent and that has bred another, now a greater daring. Any parties in doubt may see Ironside by Chuks Iloegbunam. If for any reason he cannot get a visa and see the Africana-Nigeriana Section at the British Museum, London and the Library of Congress, USA.

Achebe's is like the story of the rape victim who returned to her abuser, the rapist, hailing him for such an orgasmic sex and declaring him a lover for life and offering herself and groaning in joy, fu-k me up, you are my hero and lover for life!

Thus the two men we have listed, Shobanjo and Nwosu can arguably and representatively be the best and most statesmanlike in their trade. But are they conscious they could be the foot soldiers of a neo-imperial commercial invasion, termed branding, even if it pays so well? That is, they are the modern-day warrant chiefs, even if only in commercial terms?

9

Why The South-West Dominate The Soft-Sell Magazine

The tragedy with Nigeria, especially her loud mouthed elite, is that they are only learners and are never quite explorers and discoverers of knowledge. And this is even unto that which is specifically Nigerian. But out there in the North Americas and Europe, their attitude is decidedly different. For instance, in Sorbonne or Harvard, a tradition over-rules. That tradition is that the digestion and understanding of facts, however weighty, sinks into insignificance in comparison with the discovery of new facts and or knowledge, however trifling.

Thus the Nigerian elite goes to learn all that is known about rocket science or securitised derivatives but is completely ignorant of how to evade gun shots at Mushin or discover how to make more garri with less water and thus drive away hunger. Of course, he is a tutored expert on how to make more bread with less wheat. But there is the caveat: Africa has to import all her wheat.

So, he returns from his educational travels abroad or at home and prides himself a technocrat. But truth be told, he knows nothing except what he has been taught and explained to in Harvard, Nsukka or Oxford. Appoint him to anything and the local environment will overwhelm and battle him to the ground. In desperation if not ennui, he enjoins and joins the rest of us to give, take and eat bribes. Bribes, by the way, are Nigeria's staple menu, head and shoulders above gbegiri soup or ofe onugbu. Egunje no bi him spoil Nigeria. What spoils Nigeria is the inability of our technocratic class to meaningfully address or even raise the Nigerian question beyond their profuse copying and poaching of the Singaporeans, Malaysian and other models.

Anyway, nothing spoils. We need to help at redeeming matters and must begin a study of ourselves true to the age-old admonition: Man know thyself!

An aspect of this will come under what we call the sociology of business studies. The Turf Gamers are proud and happy to remark; we are the first to pioneer this specialty study worldwide. Doubt that? Then google it online. (The Turf Game is a column run by this author in The Sun newspaper, Nigeria. It was here that the sociology of business advantage was first officially canvassed).

Our attention today is on why and how the Yoruba/the South-West dominate and will for a longer while dominate the soft-sell newspaper industry. Meanwhile, we must remark that the reasons they dominate or don't the broadsheet or serious press is an entirely different and largely unrelated matter. We shall in due time, if we find the schedule, return to it. Now it is the soft-press ahoy.

Before we go further let us retail some anecdotes about Chief Ideh Okafor, not his real names, who is Igbo. Okafor is a billionaire and is in his late forties or early fifties. The last time I chatted with him he spoke of how he looks forward to the mother of all parties which he will host when he hits it to the grand old age of 70 – which is an Igbo celebration of coming eldership. A similar ceremony is called Ime Uke, for instance, in a town, Nkwerre in Imo State that is known to this writer. As Okafor looked so far into a future, too far away to be mapped and or planned for, I smiled. It also so happened that a certain Igbo entrepreneur/journalist marketed Chief Okafor to finance his planned soft-sell magazine. I was brought in as a consultant.

Going through the spread sheet and business plan, I smiled again. It all added up and as suggested, but that is on paper. Theoretically, the proposal will make a splash and a killing in the market place. But I thought it worthy first to listen to Chief Okafor. His worry, he told me, is that o so so ndi Yoruba ka ime paper malu aru. Translated loosely – 'it is only the Yoruba that newspapering fits as a second skin'. I smiled yet again. Of course, Okafor is mixing and merging the categories of soft and serious press on one hand, their ownership and management, and the sociology and history of media enterprise on the other, as one and the same thing. The error is understandable but much on that latter.

I knew it will not work (spread sheet's models and plans are one thing, the market and her ruling sociology yet another reality) and I told him so. I did not quite tell him why, but we will do that here. Now, since I have known Chief Okafor, despite his being a billionaire, the only parties he has hosted are those of his son's wedding, the carnival-like burial of his mother and the opening ceremony of two or three businesses he is promoting. And all these in a count of more than 10 long years and perhaps more. We are not blaming him; it is just his lifestyle and we merely record it.

Of course, he is typical of the Igbo millionaire class… its social and event lives are Spartan, especially in their numbers and even profligacy or generosities. This is especially so when compared with the Yoruba equivalents.

If Chief Okafor was a Yoruba, say an Otunba Adebiyi Gbenga Anifowoshe, for instance, it is almost certain in the 10 years we would have had parties, ceremonies counted in their tens, if not hundreds.

Before do-gooders misunderstand us, this is not a criticism or preference of either the Igbo or Yoruba sociologies. It is just a specific photographic record to be used as a tool of business analysis and explanation. So there are no prejudices… just sociological science or accounting with bias for sociology of business. Now it follows that if Otunba Gbenga has a party and partying profile of tens or hundreds in a 10-year period and Chief Okafor counted a maximum of six in the same period, a market will develop to service and supply a steady demand for parties in Otunba Gbenga's jurisdiction. This is especially indicated as there will be a million more Otunbas. Further, entrepreneurs will deconstruct the units of partying and deliver economics of specialty in those, and associated areas. That is, a supplier and sub-contractor industry will naturally emerge. The evidence is in all the great centres of specific industries have attached to them their supplier chains concerns. For example, much of the gift bread industry (achicha, ihe ahia, the commonly edible or bread is still the preferred Igbo na Oru gift form) in Onitsha is to specifically supply travellers who use Onitsha as a hub. The Japanese car manufacturing corridors are of course famous for their supplier sub-contractors. Even beyond that, social and entrepreneurial innovators will continually roll back tradition and open up to imaginative newness. The evidences are also in.

In a report The Sun of Friday, August 19, 2011 writes on the story of Royal Spices, one of Nigeria's big players in the catering and events management industry and its Chief Executive Officer, Dr. (Mrs) Olufunmi Adegbile:

> Her entry into the industry in Ibadan revolutionised the industry in these parts, in terms of quality of menu, packaging and presentation, such that her services became hotly sought after in Ibadan and its environs. The secret? Adegbile explains: "I was actually motivated into the business because I saw an opening and just wanted to fill the void.

I just realised that when I went to parties, I saw a lot of mismanaged events, poor presentation of food which I believed could be better packaged. I asked why food couldn't be cooked for 1,000 people and it would be as tasty as that cooked in the house for only four people. ...It was a time when people used iron tables, most times rusty and the food would be served on them like that. We believed the tables could be covered without the legs showing so the guests could have good appetite for food.

Again this on March 6, 2011, Nimi Akinkugbe who writes personal finance on Next had this to say on her article Saving on a shoestring; Thirty-two year old Shade lives rent free with her aunt... decided to log her expenses for the month of January 2011; it highlighted her typical monthly expense pattern.

Tithes: ₦17,000.00; Hair/Beauty: ₦32,500.00; Eating out & Entertainment; ₦30,000.00; Take-away meals; ₦20,000.00; Aso-ebi: ₦45,000.00; Mobile phone recharge cards; ₦16,000.00; Transport; ₦30,000.00; Clothes; ₦25,000.00. Total; ₦215,500.00.

Firstly, it is not likely that an Igbo lady who lives in Onitsha or Enugu will witness a quantity of partying as to suggest a business opening. It is simply that the Igbo rich who could be up to great parties are simply put not into it. One could easily notice that not only is there a budget for aso-ebi or social partying uniform and haute couture, but that category consumes the single largest allocation. Her Igbo counterpart will likely not have a monthly budget for aso-ebi and not to talk of it being the largest budget allocation.

And it is not likely that a single Igbo lady who lives rent-free with her aunt will have a budget category that reads aso-ebi; that is partying uniform. There are simply put, not enough parties and partying going on to indicate that budget heading. Any such flourish will likely come under contingencies for the single lady who is Igbo and lives in Onitsha.

It has to be understood that the abundance of numbers and volume in any given market will in itself suggest innovation/s as an entry strategy. For an entrepreneur to gain entry the cheapest way is to innovate and this not only drives the business to higher level it helps to expand and increase custom.

***

Now within the South-West (Yoruba), Agoyin women are a common currency. But it is a (supplier) business invention (innovation) of the Yoruba. The justly famous Agoyin women are commercialised caterers who have been part of the Yoruba social scene for a long time. There are no such equivalents in Igbo. Even for the rich, it is the community who in the spirit of Otu Olu Obodo (civic spiritedness) join hands to cook in the event of parties or ceremonies. But these things have long been professionalised with the Yoruba. It is now being imported into Igbo na Oru, especially for the rich and we are all happy for it. In fact, there is a brisk export or inter-regional trade for the Agoyin women all over Igbo land and it is good for the nation.

I may be wrong here, but I have discovered this; that in most ceremonies hosted by the Yoruba, there seem to be enough food however small, per attendee; and its delivery and other services to the attendees are a lot smoother than those of the Igbo. This is so even in cases where the Igbo could be comparatively richer. My thinking is that the Yoruba have been long and prodigiously at it and thereby may have developed and fine-tuned, better than the Igbo, on the management, delivery of foods and services for large crowds. The business of serving social crowds enjoys necessarily a supplier innovation premium at the Yoruba end of the market.

On the innovation side, it is the Yoruba who invented aso-ebi, that is, uniforms, as a social haute-couture and not just work or power toga. They may be the first in the world and we may have to salute them for that. Hitherto, uniforms were for serious or business-like operations like nursing, soldiering, etc., but the Yoruba devolved them into social tools, for group and individual fashion statements. (Perhaps only a Yoruba, here the irrepressible Fela Kuti, would have coined the inimitable saying; uniform na clothe na tailor dey sew am. It might also be worthy to remark that the Yoruba have one of the highest incidences of official uniforms culture than any other national group in Nigeria. In Yoruba land for instance, street side mechanics not only sow graduation uniforms or togas, they also throw big ticket freeing or graduation parties. Fela, possibly Nigeria's greatest philosopher, may have seen and counted too many uniforms to be reminded it is not a mystery but a fixture of tailors. That singular insight of Fela helped as no other to position military juntas as no greater than armed political robbers. Uniforms, of course, were what any man or group could have sown and shouldn't make a man, whether soldier or party freak a messiah. It is not likely some other non-Yoruba poet or philosopher would have had Fela's insight with similar metaphors. Uniforms convey psychological power and not also gaiety in Igbo unlike in Yoruba, say). So in some sense the Yoruba invention of aso ebi is some great innovation and achievement even if as it looks commonplace after the fact. Now all Nigerians copy the Yoruba on this. But the critical mass is still on the advantage of the Yoruba.

Even more aso-ebi has been innovated further and the trend for innovation continues. Sometimes, it varies in one event. If you asked, it is like friends of the celebrant may choose a particular colour/fabric etc., while friends of the siblings of the celebrant may choose another colour, etc. Thus if one visited a big ticket Yoruba event or party, a kaleidoscope of uniforms, colours will morph into a lovely bouquet or a flaming forest of human joy.

What we are saying is that the Yoruba are the founders of big party events as a routine part of life. (Interested parties may quickly wish to see Dr. Reuben Abati's piece at The Guardian of June 3, 2011). In their having achieved critical mass, it is likely they will be the primary source of innovation. Even the Yoruba poor or their not-too-rich have a strong sense of party and partying culture. Poor Mushin, for instance, one can profitably hazard, parties more than posh Independence Layout in Enugu and possibly more than the whole of Onitsha put together. And this is despite the bank and wealth balances being in favour of Onitsha/Enugu.

Now, not known to many, the soft-sell is an innovative opening up (or deconstructed specialisation) of the Yoruba partying culture as a routine market. That is, they are a sub-contractor industry to the people's active and running social life. In fact, it is an extension of the Yoruba oriki or those praise singer/drummers that visit even if uninvited at your events. This praise singer culture in social events, and freelancing on their own, is absent in the East. This may partly be, we guess, because the play of parties is not yet industrial as to have its own logic and life. In the South-East, if the singer is to be around he has to be so specifically hired. This is because, as we have suggested, it is still a cottage industry in all Igbo/South-East. That is, the room for sub-contractor entrepreneurship or innovation will be too limited. A certain threshold is demanded (in all extant/cottage industries) before entrepreneurs may any meaningfully muscle in even to innovate.

Immediately we understand that the soft-sell is an oriki/praise singing (and of course with yabbis/censure in between) in print then we are closer to the source of things. To repeat the soft-sell magazine is a supplier sub-specialty market need, just like the Agoyin caterers. The volume of business going on has crossed the critical threshold; that is, it is now too big to be left any proficiently to amateurs or the consumers.

To repeat all over again, it is the Yoruba who have achieved the critical mass in parties and partying. It is they that have the greater need to be reported as big boys, big gals and socialites. In fact, was it not for the English the Yoruba would have been the first to invent the word socialite? It is so native to their way of doing things some would even say thinking, so much so that every successful Yoruba man is born either a socialite or a prince.

And it is they who are likely to live as a second nature the nuances of the party circuit and how best to report it. The Igbo, with all their famed entrepreneurial gifts, will come as strangers to this business and its sociology. And like Warren Buffet and Paul Reichmann will advise, quite freely, I guess, never get into a business you do not understand. Why? And the answer is because it will ruin you.

Now journalism is not often only fine prose; it is even more so social and other contacts. And in the social pages of news reporting, contact is everything. If you are not admitted you cannot even report. And strangers are simply not invited to parties. This insight, ordinary after the fact, is what B. C. Forbes founded his media empire upon. At least, this is as was reported by the American Adam Smith, in his famous book The Money Game. Today, if a Dangote is listed as an official billionaire, and Nigeria celebrates, it is thanks to that heroic insight of the B. C. Forbes. So you cannot easily harvest from a sociology you did not and would not sow into. To be great social page reporter-creator-entrepreneurs, the Igbo may need to tamper with their sociology. If you doubt, wager but let it be your money and not my clients.

In an executive summary as it were; if a plucky Igbo media entrepreneur/journalist markets you to invest in his planned soft-sell magazine, a City People clone, say, then know it he wants to embark on perilous waters with your money. And I can assure that however brilliant his business plans, the attendant storms will see him buried in a sea of debt and ruin. Avoid him like a drowning man would want to flee from water. You did better investing your kobo in further sociological inquiries. The simple reason is that the spreadsheet, no matter how geeky, cannot obviate or annul the host or superintendent sociology. Finally for Igbo, what could be done as an enterprise remedy is known and or knowable, but is clearly beyond the cognitive resources of entrepreneurs. (Interested readers may wish to consult the essay; Why only the Americans could have invented the modern Computers in my new book; Nigeria... A Future in Ruins?). Or one should consult other appropriate quarters and or if he has the gumption, then the devil. Yes, the devil as well as the gods, knows everything. But then, this is not a referral, the choice is entirely yours. Life is often The Turf Game.

PART THREE:

PART THREE

10

Attorneys General As Fools And The Rise Of Para-History

Or Lawyers are as ignorant and certain as philosophers are wise and in doubt.

Rotimi Akeredolu-Ale, herein called Ake, bears the aristocratic carriage of a Plato and wears the mien of a Socrates. With his high cut chins and highly groomed white beards he looks and acts the parts. Our paths crossed when he was elected President of Nigerian Bar Association (NBA). But that was only via the television screens, and apparently that was enough. Of course, he bears a double barrelled surname and that suggests some storied background worth preserving. Or perhaps, as modern democratic and commercial practice will allow, it is all some invention. As the then NBA president he speaks for lawyer's trade union which perhaps makes him their wise man even if not exactly a Socrates.

On one of those TV days we met, he was so enthused and passionate, which I am told is currently the right way to behave. His claims were not only false they were possibly ignorant and outlandish. He threatened that the NBA which he led was going to open a liaison office at the National Assembly, on the very spurious ground that this [the constitution] is our document... that the constitution is a legal document and law-making is a legal process.

I think the great man is totally and completely wrong and has to be told so. The constitution is not a legal document. The constitution is a typographers' document; the constitution is a literary document; the constitution is a printers' document and the constitution is a freedom document. The constitution is also a historical and a philosophical document. And the constitution is without denying it also a legal document among other part and partisan claimants. None of these parties shall lay claim to the ownership of a document, not even in any technical sense or on the alleged ground of frequency of use. The only exclusive concession is to say that the constitution is a peoples' document. Lawyers have no special role in the making of constitutions except as draftsmen and this is if the people so wills. Otherwise their services are completely dispensable as the people deem it right. And just as lawyers use or cite the constitution in the practice of their trade, historians and others also make reference to constitutions as source or interpretative material for earning their living.

Of course, any parties interested in the history of the making of the US constitution will know that after the points were agreed upon it was specially handed to a select numbers who were thought to be felicitous with the language to couch it in memorable phrases, especially its opening lines. Today, the US constitution is used as a sample of excellent composition and source material for practice in elegant and high minded prose. Also, the same document is used to gauge how language has accreted or lost meaning over time. That it is used for the study of language and philology. Thus the idea that the constitution is a legal document in any sense other than it is only in part and as the others, is fiction.

So all the relevant and cognate professions have their claims as partisans and none may suppose that it is the first among equals or given to any special claims thereof. What the lawyers are wont to do is to corner and turn the inheritance of the many into the possession of a narrow tribe, themselves. But this is the little error of lawyers, their spurious and even fetish delusion that they have a special claim to the constitution. This false foreground of lawyers leads many lawyers into needless errors of certainty in subject matters they perhaps know so little. But given their alleged oratorical powers and professional self love, they confuse semantics with logic, arguments with assertions. By this they make their single greatest disservice to the nation. They achieve this by serving us a menu list of staple ignorance that is as nation-killing as it is wondrous. We shall examine a list of them taking our servings from senior and prominent lawyers.

Let us quote Ake; *I don't think there is anything wrong with Nigeria's constitution. I think it is all right; the problem is with the people handling the constitution. The problem is Nigerians and majorly of the problem is that we don't have leaders who can motivate the people, and as long as that is lacking, the people are not motivated for that long the country will remain retarded and we will have retrogression.* **(The Punch, January 16, 2011)**

In a supporting motion, as it were, Chief Richard Akinjide contributes:

> *I feel very sad and embarrassed that in the last 45 years, we have had more than five constitutions but the critical point is that nothing is wrong with our constitution but our rulers. If you bring Americans here to operate this constitution, it would work. And in the same vein, if you take Nigerians to America, you will find out that the constitution there will not work for them.*
>
> *In the past eight years, what we had in Nigeria was a military government masquerading as a civilian government. And let me correct one thing which most Nigerians do not know. When we drafted the 1979 constitution, what came out was not what we submitted. Then Gen. Olusegun Obasanjo (the Head of State) did 17 critical amendments. We should stop comparing the American constitution with ours... the problem of the country is enormous and the problem is neither political nor economic but it is a human problem, and until we solve that human problem, we will not progress. It is ironic that those who don't know are governing those who know.* **(The Guardian, October 3, 2007)**

Expectedly, Akinjide's has a lot of historical fibre, giving throwaways that may under cross examination annul his assertions. We may just briefly conclude with these two lawyers' claims by observing 'that there is nothing wrong with the Nigerian constitution is almost a universal fixture with them, especially those we may call the Kings College Club of lawyers.' These two big forensic minds are just representative names and are here no guiltier or any less innocent.

The first question to ask is, what leads lawyers to this error? The answer is their assertion that the constitution is a legal document. This very absurd claim seduces most of our TV anchor men and women to call in lawyers almost exclusively when there is a constitutional and even legal problem. But like we have warned, the constitution is not a legal document. It is that and is also as relevant here as a historical document.

So, in historical and historicist terms one can ask, is there anything wrong with the Nigerian constitution? And even more importantly in freedom and philosophical terms, is there anything wrong with the Nigerian constitution? And we contend that in the context of human freedom and the historical march to human civilization, that there is everything wrong with the Nigerian constitution. In fact, in those terms it can summarily be said that Nigeria has no constitution at all and thus the question, if anything is wrong with the Nigerian constitution, may be superfluous.

Let us absolve ourselves of the complications of racial separateness. From Moses in the wilderness of Canaan proclaiming laws to fellow Jews and converts under the self-invented claim, 'thus said the lord your God☐ to the gathering of some of the most historic men at Philadelphia in 1787, passing through Magna Carta and others, it is one single continuous march of man in search of liberty, freedom and rights. If, as a historian, you cannot link the threads, then you have failed in your principal task which is the recognition that the human story is one epic even if with several dramatic personae and acts and not an unrelated series of episodes like it were of the Tower of Babel. If a historian fails in this then he is confusing the status report with the trend dynamics. And the two are not one.

So, what a great and gifted statesman should do, aided by fine and able historians, is to track the positive trends and take things to their limits or next levels. The example of what the men who wrote the American constitution did is instructive and that alone confirms the American constitution is a historical document among other qualifying epithets. For them their task was to be heirs to the finest traditions of man in search for freedom, for redemption, for civilization and our speculated evolution to godhood.

Here I am in total agreement with the word an Akinjide uses, invent. As a writer I would have preferred the phrase, and they stretched the lineage and line of their inheritance from the past to link the golden future they dreamed and desired. This is to hint at this historical continuity that often escapes the lawyerly mind.

But imbedded in this historicity is a fact that is often lost to Nigerian lawyers in their ignorant certainty. It is the single greatest phrase ever uttered by the modern man as a historical being. Before America there was no such phrase in history and it may in justice be considered sacred. It is: We the people... in order to form a more perfect Union... and secure the Blessings of Liberty to ourselves and to our Posterity, do ordain and establish this Constitution....

The key words showcase not only the historicity but the ambition to further history. It was the first time a people were founding themselves into a nation by themselves and not just by their leaders or guardians or mere historical accidents. And their vision is to form a more perfect union that is historically improving on the unions that then existed before them; that is, the nations of Europe. The nations and boundaries of Europe were cut and cast through accidents, conquests, consolidations and treaties, but were over and sometimes against the will of the people. It was this historical error of Europe that cost them dearly and engendered separatist movements, which were sometimes resolved by the historical accidents, that America pre-empted by the greatest gift to modern man; 'we the people'. Even the phrase 'and secure the blessings of liberty' is not a vain flourish. It is an outgrowth from the history of much of the then Europe where parliaments, kings, the plebeians, etc were all securing and loosing liberty and tyranny successively.

The Nigerian constitution therefore failed completely in its essential duty which was to consolidate and further advance the course of human freedom, progress and civilization and not just create a lawyerly jurisdiction or document. That is, the Nigerian so-called constitution failed as a historical document. That is, it has no validity in time and therefore in space. Historically, Nigeria has no constitution.

And how did it do that? It excluded the 'we the people' from the nation. What remained were lawyers to the military dictators, a few plutocrats and their wives, armed robbers, concerned professionals, human right profiteers and deal makers, fools and everybody else 'but we the people'. Of course' the assumption is that these men, the Akinjides, the Akeredolus are the wise men? But if one read the American contributions to human freedom, pursuit of civilization and its period history well, one salient fact emerges. It is that the American constitution is a historical improvement on hitherto existing constitutions. This crucial improvement may be stated; that a democracy is neither the rule by, nor is it by the rules set by the especially wise or those who so claim or pay PR people to so assert, that they are the wisest since King Solomon. So the first act of the democratic order which is authoring a constitution is the peoples' sole rite and must be returned to them or all purported processes in its stead come to nothing or annul themselves. This is the philosophical underlay of a democracy, its para-history as it were. Anything outside it is a dictatorship by other names and these lawyers must be condemned for abetting and aiding such blood sucking partisanships. Even if it is legally sound it is historically and philosophically dubious to have consented so. So to say that there is nothing wrong with our constitution is fashionable ignorance at best, besides other charges of arrogance and even historical perjury or lying against history that may be heaped against it.

This, of course, is without prejudice to the lawyerly claims that if a dictator establishes a republic and secures it, then business must go on. It does not matter if the dictator was and still is a practising armed or highway/political robber. The important thing for the lawyers is that there is order and not civilization. We are not moralists; we are only living men, so we have no assertions against the business must go on thesis of the lawyers. Our concern is that the facts be put in the public domain. While lawyers are certain business must go on with the order securing dictator, the philosophers are in doubt if it is right. Wondering further, is it even right and moral to be alive and well in our modern era breathing under the guns of a dictator? Meanwhile, the lawyers are ahead of the rat race and against the human race. For them anywhere there is and can be a brief, there then is the rule of law. And if we let them they may even say a civilization. As long as you can sue and be sued, then all is well and the world is round. That is a lawyerly confession

Similar to the error of the lawyerly assertion that the constitution can be written by unelected wise men is their assertion that every country has its history and therefore whatever and however it does it is right. They go further to cite their staple; that the British have no written constitution yet it is a model of good governance. This too is historical ignorance masquerading as forensic certainty. Firstly, what is this noise about the British not having a written constitution?

Are the British only such historical societies? The answer is, of course, no. Just down here at the Benin kingdom they run a firm and working non-written constitution. The historical even if not legal question to ask is, why. The answer will drive the enquirer from the status report of an un-written constitution to the trend which we may now characterize as the historical fact or truth. It is not enough to accumulate the bill and quantities, one must also have the vision and fluidity of the architect to turn the ponderous facts and incidents into and towering structures.

The example of the Benin kingdom is occasioned by the absence of literacy skills among the ancient Benins. They, like almost the rest of us, had no written language. But they ran their kingdom ably and the result shows. In its last 100 or so years history, for instance, there has not been any record of jerks in the transfer of power from one Oba/king to another, which is a crucial measure of the stability and health of political systems. Every traditional Benin power player seems to know his place and keeps to it. There is no greater un-written constitution.

What happened to the Benin is essentially what happened to the British in trend analysis even if not status reports. The very idea of a constitution, we have to understand, is an innovation. The word constitution did not pre-exist time. Men invented it and by need and vision.

Societies were all ruled by memory of traditions and the wisdom of their wise men. But with skills in writing these memories of traditions and postulations of the wise got codified and were reasonably well preserved and able to be made reference to. We may quickly recall that Socrates objected to things being written thinking among other things that it will weaken the memory of young men.

Writing is thus a tool of super-human memory and keeper of tradition. So that the British have no written constitution has no meaning other than that she is a naturally and slowly evolved society. It is her body of written or recorded rules, scattered through her historical and other records which in Benin is preserved in the memory of their wise, songs, proverbs that guide the political and other conducts of the British. If Benin were as literate as the British they too would have had an un-written constitution in the manner of the British. The paradox of an unwritten British constitution is a paradox till you abandon your legal certainties and open her up to historical and other cognate enquiries. Of course, the constitution, as we are saying, is not merely a legal documentation. Even to fully understand constitutions you must bring in the legal, the historical, the philosophical, the typographical, and the orthographical. Otherwise you will have the certainty of the presumptuous compounded by avoidable ignorance. And today I am almost certain that aspects of the Benin tradition are now in written and palace-authorised forms. They with their other traditions make up the unwritten Benin constitution and the document works.

Thus an unwritten constitution is a historical or technical handicap and not a legal choice. And to understand this we must repudiate the presumptuous though popular ignorance that the constitution is a legal document. Certain constitutional complications are resolvable at levels other than the merely legal. Before the American written constitution, constitutions only happened and were incidented or accumulated piece by piece.

What the Americans achieved in writing down a constitution was orthographically as revolutionary as the invention of the wheel. That is, we must come to knowledge that the concept of a written constitution is in itself a revolution. Before the wheel, men moved their loads but the wheel made the task a lot easier. Before America, men had written (un-written for non-literate societies like the Benins) laws, customs that guided them but those were scattered in documents as far apart in time and themes as Moses and Shakespeare on one hand and Aesop's fables and Plato's Republic on the other. The revolutionary magic of bringing them or aspects of them, under one roof or cover has to be appreciated even as it appears so commonplace today.

We may all quickly recall the denigration of attempts to publish the classics in paperback form. In fact, many concluded that in being cheap paperback a classic is no longer a classic. It is a claim similar to the assertion that Things Fall Apart in soft cover is inferior to Things Fall Apart in hard cover.

So the American experience in constitution writing was a historical landmark and improvement on the history of constitutions via its orthography, its content, its packaging, possibly in its legal content. It is similar with what happened with banks, words and orthographies. Banks started as depositories and evolved to be credit creating and granting institutions.

Also as was originally, words were invented to record and retrieve extant and important thoughts and possibly record of events. The history of the preservation of Islam□s holy book is largely instructive here. Later words leaped off its original aim and were now to be used to invent new thought forms and categories. That is, as we have earlier hinted, written words were invented to aid and replace memory. And men invented it further to help invent new thoughts and this second line invention led to the first explosion in knowledge, just as there was in bank credit creation by the further development of the concept of banking. And American banks improving on their British inheritance are simply better at credit administration and creation and therefore entrepreneurial incubation. Silicon Valley is in part the creation of American bankers inheriting but transcending their British bankerly traditions.

And invention never finishes. So ours is to continue on the line of inventions and not be looking back in lawyerly ignorance to justify even if in part, our tragic present. The issue and question should not be whether the British operates an unwritten constitution but what is our historical inheritance from all around the world and what can we do to earn it? And we must earn it for it to work with us at all. You cannot outsmart history as some of our military junta heads of state were often deluded. And that is, as we have earlier canvassed, earning our place in history is strictly by innovation and not in founding justification by the past of our evolutionary (political) ancestors. My fear is that our lawyers in the tradition of the King's College we are the heirs are incapable of original thoughts or breakthrough thinking. Theirs is to inherit the British and whichever other civilization that they can purloin. So their plan is to convert their learning and their being called to make public roads into private ruling thrones and palaces. The accusation is not mine. I am actually adapting from Christopher Okigbo. And tragically they have the collaboration of their other intellectual king's men. But if they share the meat let them remember thunder.

Even worse is the now fashionable phrase among our lawyers arguing about some constitutional matters. I have heard them ask on many occasions what are the intentions of the framers of the [Nigerian] constitution. One, the phrase applies to Nigeria and her constitution is meaningless philosophically, philologically, and historically. And properly should not have any legal meaning. It is an ignorant mimicking of their American counterpart at its very basics and essentials utterly different. When Americans ask what are the intentions of the framers of the given constitutional line they mean the following; this is a constitution authored by our ancestors representing us. And in our being their inheritors and legatees in law and in history, philosophy and ethics, therefore we are as they were, the co-authors of the American constitution. It is our living document, our (not their) collective will and creation. However, the minds of the people, that is; we the people, had to be bound up in words and phrases. To bridge the gap between putting the minds of the people into the words of men (as appointed to the task) has always been a challenge. So since the authors wished for the good of themselves, (and that is representatively, in law and in existence, us their legatees and inheritors), we their legatees can now ask what is it we would have written in the light of today? That is, we are the authors, because the constitution, in being a living document, is framed for men and not for governments. The authorship of that constitution is extant as it passes into historical, philosophical and legal inheritance of every new American generation. That is, again, if we wish good of ourselves, what is today's equivalence of that wish?

To make it look concrete, accountants and economists calculate the future values of Naira. What does one Naira today amount to tomorrow adjusting for inflation and interest? Or what is today's value for one Naira of yesterday? The key but here largely unstated phrase is; the we, the authors as against those we elected to help us frame the constitution are the people at play and who seek current equivalent of our rights or Naira values.

The intention of the framers is to represent our minds the authors, but as Okigbo once rightly observed, and there are the errors of rendering. The question is asked at all as an attempt to eliminate the gap between the pen of the renderers and the minds of renderees; that is, those whose minds are being rendered. And that is again we the people! Or in using Christopher Okigbo's phrase to eliminate or adjust for the errors of rendering in more modern speak. It therefore follows that if there is not a we; that is, the authors of the constitution, delegating the task of the constitution being written and framed, there cannot be the framers in any meaningful, philosophical, historical and even communal sense anymore. It therefore follows that a constitution written by a gang, no matter how wise and or all powerful, cannot in any meaningful sense be elevated or legitimatised with the phrase, what are the intentions of the framers. This is because they framed it for themselves, over and above us the people and at their own election. We the people did not delegate them and have nothing in real terms to do with their misplaced patriotic effusions or other pretensions. If ever anybody is a patriot let him subject himself to the peoples' democratic choice. Anything outside this is historical and even commonsensical insanity, even if it makes legal sense allegedly.

And the Attorneys General that ran with dictators wearing their wisdom wigs are actually fools. First, their assumption is that you can bear a gun against the peoples' will and be civilised. Perhaps, one has put things too strongly but perhaps again these things needed to be put in such violent style if only to save our future. And let the attorney general who consorts with the armed political robber know that he is fooling nobody and that he too is a receiver of stolen office. Bearing guns and wearing wigs should not go together. And that cannot make one a patriot.

In the case of a constitution written by the self or dictator appointed wise or the armed and pretender nationalists, you ask, what are the intentions of the authors who are also the framers and even finishers of the laws. The truth is that the military usurper-dictator General Abubakar Abdulsalami and his un-elected and, as it appears, unelectable military junta-dictatorship are the authors, the framers and the finishers of that decreed constitution. That they acted in cahoots with lawyers does not make it legal to the extent that the people may countenance it. It therefore follows that you speak of the intentions of the authors who also are her framers and finishers. And since there is an overlapping of the authors, the framers and the finishers, the question of intentions do and should not arise at all. You may now choose other phrases and words like what would the people and or their delegates have written? Or you have the courage to ask, what did a General Abdulsalam mean for us by this mystifying or even accursed phrase? And or perhaps go to Abdulsalam and ask him, what are your intentions here for yourself and the rest of your people which does not include 'we the people'?

Unlike with the American, there is no gap between these Nigerian counterpart characters to warrant the asking ourselves the question at all. These men are acting like Hammurabi who believed God called on him to write what today will have been called Abdulsalami constitution. But we ask, do these men have the wisdom of Hammurabi and did their fathers bequeath them an empire and, worse, are we their chattels? What is the relationship between Nigerians and Abdulsalami, on one hand, and his guns, on the other? And for how long shall it subsist? Have we been conned for eternity by a gun-totting General? Or it is just that perhaps we lack the courage to say no in thunder? But thank God there are other ways and one can justly wonder what fools we are when folks appear troubled why it is the country is going down. Where else do want this country to go? What is our portion in upholding an armed and a forged constitution? Are we children of prostitutes or did we not suckle our mothers' breasts? How come we behave like beasts? Or is our lot (not) the same as the Jews in the land of Pharaoh? How can we support in peace what Abdulsalam scammed us out in war? We do not owe him that allegiance. A coup is an undeclared war raging over and against the people. We have to put an end to our animalisation by and from Nzeogwu to Abdulsalami and reclaim our humanity whole and intact. Without freedom life is not worth a breath. Then you can die and be free and freed. Freed at least from the humiliation of living in the era of internet, iPod, sagging... hi-hop, jazz freedoms, by a constitution written by gun-bearers with dead brains, (and if you have sharp and living brains argue your case) who think there is innocence in brute strength and forged even fraudulent wigs of wisdom.

But you do not draft constitutions without freedom and with abridged franchise. In modern philosophical speak that is meaningless. Constitutions are written by the people. Anyway, if constitutions are to be obeyed by the people they the people must write and author it. Otherwise you need a policing and policed state of the apartheid era type to keep the constitution working. It just does not make economic sense to have a police state. That is why it is more efficient (the economics of constitutions) to allow the people to write their constitution. The cost of running an armoured or forged constitution, as Nigeria has shown, is not worth the effort. Today, despite what teary-eyed philosophers hold, it is moral and philosophically legal to steal, to rob and do whatever you can since the constitution itself is a fraud and a forged document. It therefore allows us to do as we want so long as we can go free. Is this the country we want as designed by our Attorneys General and the armoured tank Generals? I beg if una mama no born una well, my mama born me well jareh!

Now it is not essential that American historians and or philosophers know some of these things. In fact, they do not need to know. It is the duty of the provincial who is about to inquire and adapt the metropolitan civilization and ways to study and unravel all what it is that makes America (or the West), that the Americans would not and oftentimes cannot know. This is what we will call para-history. Alfred Whitehead, mathematician and one of the finest historical minds, first pointed out the troubling but exact insight to us.

If one is investigating a past and an extant civilization one should look beyond and besides their historians□ record of themselves. Often the vitality of a culture and civilization is assumed away or neglected as too obvious by its on-shore or in-house chroniclers. For example, it has been noted that there is no mention of camels in a certain sacred title which is the Arab book par excellence. If you miss this para-history as our lawyers all seem to, you come to being nothing other than a police report journalist or historian. And that is why the newspapers are soon lost to time but the scriptures, the Bible, the Ofo remaineth.

So to achieve a great and therefore usable form of American history we must return to Mother Aendu's phrase; this history is new, is indeed news! That is, inventing ancient and already known history to be new yet truthful. That is, to look for that in ancient or contemporary history, that redeeming aspect that is hidden and unknown to her enactors and is new, and is news. That is, to teach Americans their own history in the light of our inheritance of their own and now our pursuit of our own civilization.

And the phrase re-echoes, what are the intentions of the framers of the constitution now to be inherited by us as a part of the larger human and not the tinier American family. That which is American is also human and therefore inheritable by us or just about any other human society. But to come to legitimate and not false inheritance you must pay certain voluntary historical ground rent and innovation fees. And that rent is in the correct interpretation of para-history and not police report history which lawyers, to be fair to them, are apparently used to.

As we can see, in the certainty of our lawyers there are errors and with it their uncanny attempt to pass off as philosophers while earning their briefs. No other professions and professionals have done greater damage to the Nigerian nation than lawyers acting as Attorneys General to dictators, who are really nothing but armed robbers even if only the political kind.

The question that must be asked is, why are our lawyers prone to such errors? The answer is given by Erelu Dr. Olusola Obada ex-Deputy Governor of Osun State; to tell the truth, lawyers make the best politician because they have an insight into almost everything... Perhaps, the only profession a lawyer cannot be engaged in is surgery! (Vanguard, June 28, 2009)

The question next follows; what are lawyers taught at school that they have an insight into everything and not their ignorance? Yet knowing what you do not know is the first primer to all insights. Then there is an urgent need for a total revamp of the curriculum besides other things before they kill us with their legal all too legal, fraudulent insight.

POSTCRIPT

Attorneys General as Fools

*Our saving task is to philosophise history,
and not to historicise philosophy. History is
a lousy and lazy man's philosophy... and philosopher.*
-Mother A'endu

On July 29, 2011 The Telegraph of London ran a report. It is worth quoting in some detail: Iceland reviews constitution with help from online community.

Tiny but tech-savvy Iceland is overhauling its constitution in the wake of an economic catastrophe and has turned to the internet to get input from citizens.

The 25-member council drafting the new constitution is reaching out to Icelanders online, especially through social media sites Facebook and Twitter, video-sharing site YouTube and photo site Flicker.

Iceland's population of 320,000 is among the world's most computer-literate. Two-thirds of Icelanders are on Facebook, so the constitutional council's weekly meetings are broadcast live on the social networking site as well as on the council's website.

"It is possible to register through other means, but most of the discussion takes place via Facebook," said Berghildur Bernhardsdottir, spokesman for the constitutional review project.

When the North Atlantic island nation gained independence from Denmark in 1944, it simply took the Danish constitution and made a few minor adjustments, such as substituting the word "president" for "king."

A thorough review of the constitution has been on the agenda ever since, but action came only after the crisis in 2008, when Iceland's main commercial banks collapsed within a week, the kroner currency plummeted and protests toppled the government.

"To me, it has long been clear that a comprehensive review of the constitution would only be carried out with the direct participation of the Icelandic people," said Iceland's Prime Minister Johanna Sigurdardottir, one of the champions of the constitutional review since taking office in 2009.

She says it is a "distinct possibility" that the draft constitution will be put to the people in a referendum before Iceland's parliament debates final approval.

The 25 members of the constitutional council were elected by popular vote from a field of 522 candidates aged 18 and over. The council is basing its work on a 700-page report prepared by a committee that took into account the findings of 950 randomly selected Icelanders - the National Forum - who met for a day to discuss the division of powers, conservation and protection, foreign relations and more.

But, the internet component is still the most direct route for most Icelanders to weigh in. Members of the public must provide their names and addresses, and can then submit online recommendations, which are approved by local staff to avoid Internet heckling. The ideas are then passed on to the council, and are open for discussion online.

http://www.telegraph.co.uk/news/worldnews/europe/iceland/8567224/Iceland-reviews-constitution-with-help-from-online-community.html

To understand what is happening, it is important to see that online facility is an evolution of the autographical/thought storage system, just like the chalk and slate were also evolutionary ancestors of paper and the pen. And the long disc to the compact disc. The two are essentially music or sound storage facilities and have to be understood in their evolutionary terms, above all. Of course, it all started with the human memory and voice, which are data storage and recall tools. History is meaningless if it is only dates and not trends. If one is blind to or cannot find the trends embedded in or lost to the mountainous heap of data, then one cannot be deemed a historian. One is possibly a librarian, a curator and not very useful asset in these matters.

Perhaps, our inability to understand the evolutionary trends, status and state of society is accountable by the fact that we were not a part of the enactors of the development of modern society, which we freely appropriate. In the West the cognitive challenges come easier, therefore the data, facts easily flow and there is the link. Additionally, the schools in the West are full of historical traditions, dates, linkages and remembrances. From the science, literature, religion, commemorations are made of Nth birthday of a Newton, a Luther, a Goethe and even some of the key books or incidences in their lives.

In Nigeria nobody remembers anything, or is it there is nothing to remember? The matter is made worse by the fact that we are inheritors or consumers of Western ideals, goods and services. So we have no idea how those were achieved. For us a constitution is a document. It is a legal text, and might have fallen from heaven without any history. Perhaps, that is because in Europe constitutions have stabilized and seem as ahistorical as air. But we are not Europe and must understand formally that which they lived as routine lives.

In these European societies the constitution is a guide document, but it has a history, a how and why it came to be. We seem to be ignorant of those and to remain common consumers of constitutions without any ability to reverse-engineer her or her historical processes. Our lawyers, Attorneys General are no better than the ordinary Nigerian consumer who acquires a luxury motor car. Readily he has no idea it is mathematics and physics at work. It is just that he is wealthy enough to purchase the produce of another man's brains. It is true one acknowledges he need not have an idea how a motor car moves. But the same caveat cannot be granted an engineer or one who styles himself as one. The constitution is the motor car of society. So a lawyer who thinks it is only a document, any document, without knowledge it is history, philosophy, procedures at play, is a crass consumer, is like a street side mechanic. It is the scriptural tragedy of giving that which is holy to the dogs.

Perhaps, this is illustrated by the example of a village boy, we all are, who after a career life shaped by villagism, as it were, is elected to run a megacity. Of course, a megacity is something outside his experience and imagination. So conceptually he reduces it to the parameters of this hamlet. This dichotomy of the village boy running a megacity, to give one example, is what jolts the cognition out of our brains. And almost to the last, Nigerian military dictators were villagists who shot their ways through with guns, to run an entire country, indeed a sub-empire as Britain founded Nigeria. One perceptive writer has a handle on it. He calls them the Bida/provincial boys as against the Barewa/cosmopolitan boys. Immediately power left Barewa and berthed in Bida, provincialisms of mind, ideas, ideals, and accomplishments took over the national stage and psyche. And the lawyers, pretending to knowledge, only added to the darkness and ruin of all things while dressed up in their wisdom wigs.

The Nigerian tragedy may amount to naught other than the cognitive equivalent of culture shock or better block. We consequentially suffer a mental block and this incapacitates our ability to appreciate both our past and those of other nations or persons we may need to interact or borrow from.

It therefore has to be seen that the fact of the British having an unwritten constitution should be seen for what it is; an autographical development/evolution state and stage, as it were, rather than something of a spellbounding mystery, so unique, it is like two moons lighting up one night. It never happened before and will never happen again, in kind or style. No, the fact of the so-called unwritten British constitution is a historical and evolutionary commonplace. It is nothing magical at least in evolutionary and trend analysis terms. That our lawyers don't know doesn't incriminate us.

The British constitution, it must then be understood, just had to be unwritten as it were. This is because they were the founders of modern constitutionalism. On the founding of such a revolutionary concept, which for the first time in history developed the idea and practice of constitutional monarchy, it would not have been on the cards to write it out, all in one neat book. The idea of writing out in a bound and or bound-able document is itself a revolution and must be so understood. And too many revolutions cannot be carried on in one historical moment. It was therefore left for the Americans to be partakers of the British revolutionary constitutionalism, by going to the next level. And this next level is documenting it in one fixed or fixable form. And if we do not understand this we will make the error of taking them as separate revolutions. No, they are one long search for freedom, triggered by the ancient Greeks. However, it should be put on record that the more ancient Igbo in their Oru na Igbo delineation and more importantly in their design of the metaphysical universe along Ofo na Ogu also set institutional and constitutional bounds to the exercise of power. In fact, they pre-empted kings and therefore tyrannies. If you miss the trends, your dates and data are of no use even to you or the devil.

Perhaps, too, we have to understand that there are certain things that are denied every protagonist by the rites of being first. Were it otherwise no subsequent parties or concepts, would have been worthy heirs as American republicanism is worthy of British constitutional monarchy. The genius is to be worthy heirs; that is, worthy to inherit a father, an ancestor or whatever is in the public domain.

What this means is that if you did not have the revolutionary content of your father in you, that is, the ability to do all he did if you were his own father, then you are not a worthy son; and whether or not you know it you are really out of inheritance. One of the best examples in history is in the inheritance lineage of Socrates, Plato and Aristotle. None of these men stopped at his inheritance, which was one of the greatest ever. In fact, each improved all he inherited so dramatically that one can speak of them as the equal co-founders of Western philosophy. It is certain also the order is not relevant. If we imagined that Aristotle had come first, and had fathered Socrates and Socrates, Plato, it is almost certain these imagined sons of Aristotle, that is Socrates and Plato, would have done great revolutionary things, with their inheritance of the first big mind, the imaginary Aristotle.

Perhaps, we close the essay by quoting the Harvard philosopher, Peter Ludlow: Far from being absurd, the idea that the Constitution is a living organism follows from the fact that the words used in writing the Constitution are underdetermined and dynamic and thus "living organisms" in the metaphorical sense in play here. In this respect, there is nothing unique about the Constitution. It is a dynamic object because of the simple reason that word meanings are dynamic. Every written document — indeed every word written or uttered — is a living organism. (The New York Times, April 22, 2012)

The author closes in on the very evolutionary nature of words, the words themselves, by which we write our constitutions. Even words are themselves under evolutionary/revolutionary challenges, changes and growth. And these need to be understood.

Printed in the United States
By Bookmasters